TRENDS IN WELFARE, WORK AND THE ECONOMIC WELL-BEING OF FEMALE-HEADED FAMILIES WITH CHILDREN

Trends in Welfare, Work and the Economic Well-Being of Female-Headed Families with Children

Thomas Gabe

Novinka Books
New York

Senior Editors: Susan Boriotti and Donna Dennis
Coordinating Editor: Tatiana Shohov
Office Manager: Annette Hellinger
Graphics: Wanda Serrano
Editorial Production: Vladimir Klestov, Matthew Kozlowski and Maya Columbus
Circulation: Ave Maria Gonzalez, Vera Popovic, Luis Aviles, Raymond Davis, Melissa Diaz and Jeannie Pappas
Communications and Acquisitions: Serge P. Shohov
Marketing: Cathy DeGregory

Library of Congress Cataloging-in-Publication Data

ISBN: 1-59033-508-2

Copyright © 2003 by Novinka Books, An Imprint of
Nova Science Publishers, Inc.
400 Oser Ave, Suite 1600
Hauppauge, New York 11788-3619
Tele. 631-231-7269   Fax 631-231-8175
e-mail: Novascience@earthlink.net
Web Site: http://www.novapublishers.com

All rights reserved. No part of this book may be reproduced, stored in a retrieval system or transmitted in any form or by any means: electronic, electrostatic, magnetic, tape, mechanical photocopying, recording or otherwise without permission from the publishers.

The authors and publisher have taken care in preparation of this book, but make no expressed or implied warranty of any kind and assume no responsibility for any errors or omissions. No liability is assumed for incidental or consequential damages in connection with or arising out of information contained in this book.

This publication is designed to provide accurate and authoritative information with regard to the subject matter covered herein. It is sold with the clear understanding that the publisher is not engaged in rendering legal or any other professional services. If legal or any other expert assistance is required, the services of a competent person should be sought. FROM A DECLARATION OF PARTICIPANTS JOINTLY ADOPTED BY A COMMITTEE OF THE AMERICAN BAR ASSOCIATION AND A COMMITTEE OF PUBLISHERS.

Printed in the United States of America

CONTENTS

Preface		vi
Chapter 1	Introduction	1
Chapter 2	Overview	5
Chapter 3	Single Mothers' Employment Rates	9
Chapter 4	Welfare Receipt among Single Mothers	11
Chapter 5	Poor Single Mothers' Work and Welfare Status	15
Chapter 6	Effects of Earnings, Transfers, and Taxes on Single Mothers' Poverty Status	19
	Effect of Earnings and other Nonwelfare Cash Income on Poverty	20
	Effect of Cash Welfare on Poverty	22
	The Effect on Poverty of Counting Selected Income Sources not Included in the "Official" Poverty Measure	22
Chapter 7	Degree of Poverty among Poor Single Mothers	25
	Sources and Level of Income among Lower-Income Single Mothers	28
	Conclusions and Policy Implications	32
Appendix A	Cash Welfare Under-Reporting on the CPS	37
Appendix B	Family Income to Poverty Ration – Cutoffs for Income Quintiles	39
Appendix C	Support Tables	45
Index		55

PREFACE

Welfare reform legislation, signed into law in 1996 as the Personal Responsibility and Work Opportunity Reconciliation Act (PRWORA) (P.L. 104-193), replaced the 61 year-old Aid to Families with Dependent Children (AFDC) program, a federal entitlement program for low-income families with children. In place of AFDC, the law created the Temporary Assistance for Needy Families (TANF) program, a federal block grant program providing resources to the states. T ANF eliminated the federal entitlement to assistance that existed under AFDC and gave states increased flexibility to run programs to assist needy families with children. A major purpose of TANF is to end dependence of needy families on government assistance by promoting job preparation, work, and marriage.

This chapter examines trends in welfare, work and economic well-being of female-headed families with children, the principal group affected by the replacement of AFDC with TANF. The chapter presents analysis of 13 years of U.S. Census Bureau Current Population Survey (CPS) data, the principal source of information for U.S. family income and poverty statistics. The beginning of the analysis period precedes the Family Support Act of 1988, the last major nationwide welfare reform law passed by Congress before TANF. The analysis spans the run-up in welfare caseloads that began in 1989 and the historic caseload declines that have followed since reaching an all-time high in early 1994. Over the period studied, a variety of economic, demographic, and public policy and program changes, besides TANF, are likely to have affected welfare, work and the economic well-being of single-mother families. This section does not attempt to untangle these possible effects.

The analysis shows that there has been a dramatic transformation with regard to welfare, work and poverty status of single mothers over the past 13 years. Many of these changes began before the passage and implementation of TANF, but have continued, perhaps to an even greater extent, since. The analysis shows that single mothers are more likely to be working in recent than in past years, and that they are less likely to receive cash welfare or to be poor. However, reductions in poverty have not been as large as the large declines in welfare and the increased rates of work that have occurred. The analysis indicates that welfare receipt rates among *poor* families headed by single mothers have dropped considerably. Among single mothers whose incomes place them in the bottom fifth of all such mothers, income from earnings supplemented by the Earned Income Tax Credit (EITC) has grown markedly since 1993 but has failed to offset concurrent losses in cash welfare and food stamp benefits. While single mothers are less dependent on welfare in most recent than in past years, increased work has not resulted in marked gains in net income for these lowest-income families. The chapter suggests that full-time full-year work may be necessary, but not sufficient, to raise single mothers' family incomes above poverty. U.S. income support policy will continue to be challenged to promote economic self-support through work and to reduce poverty and welfare dependency among families headed by single mothers.

Chapter 1

INTRODUCTION

Welfare reform legislation, signed into law in 1996, as the Personal Responsibility and Work Opportunity Reconciliation Act (PRWORA) (P.L. 104-193), replaced the 61 year-old Aid to Families with Dependent Children (AFDC) program, a federal entitlement program to low-income families with children. In place of AFDC, the law created the Temporary Assistance for Needy Families (TANF) program, a federal block grant program to states. The AFDC program principally assisted low-income single-parent families, mostly headed by women. Federal law established the rules by which families might be determined eligible for assistance under AFDC, although states set their own benefit standards. TANF eliminated the federal entitlement to assistance that existed under AFDC, and gave states increased flexibility to design programs to assist needy families with children. A major purpose of TANF is to end dependence of needy families on government assistance by promoting job preparation, work, and marriage. Among its provisions, the federal welfare reform law imposes a maximum 5-year lifetime limit on receipt of federally-funded assistance (states may impose shorter limits than the federal maximum), and work participation requirements. A variety of groups are monitoring state programs under TANF, and the possible effects on vulnerable populations of TANF and other welfare policy changes enacted in PRWORA.

This chapter examines trends in welfare, work and economic well-being of female-headed families with children, the principal group affected by the replacement of AFDC with TANF. The chapter presents data from Congressional Research Service (CRS) analysis of U.S. Bureau of the Census March Current Population Survey (CPS), the principal source of information for U.S. family income and poverty statistics. The analysis is based on CPS data collected from March 1988 to March 2000. The earliest year's data precedes the passage of the Family Support Act of 1988 (P.L. 100-485), the last major nationwide attempt prior to TANF to reform the AFDC program. The data series begins before the most recent run-up in cash welfare caseloads that occurred under AFDC in the late-1980s and early 1990s, continues through the period in which caseloads peaked (March 1994), and follows through the most recent period of caseload declines, which, as of this date, continue.

Over the period examined in this section, a variety of economic and demographic factors, and policy interventions are generally thought to have affected cash welfare caseloads. Increased numbers of single-mother families, especially never-married mothers who are prone to poverty and receipt of welfare, as well as the economic recession (July 1990 to March 1991) are generally thought to have contributed to the increase in the AFDC caseload from mid-1989 to March 1994.[1] The current economic expansion (since March 1991), the longest in U.S. history, has presented a most favorable economic climate to provide jobs to mothers who otherwise might rely on welfare.

A variety of welfare policy interventions are likely to have affected welfare caseloads by conditioning benefits on new behavioral requirements. For example, the 1988 Family Support Act extended work requirements (which could include work preparation activities, such as education and training) from mothers with child as young as 6 to mothers with a child as young as 3 (under the law, states had the option of extending work requirements to mothers with a child as young as 1). In the years immediately preceding passage of the 1996 welfare law, states experimented with changes to welfare policy permitted by the Secretary of the Department of Health and Human Services (DHHS).[2] Among the features of state programs tested under waiver authority granted by the Secretary were efforts to strengthen work requirements, experiments requiring a "work first" approach rather than "training first, followed by work", time limits, strengthened sanctions for noncompliance with welfare rules, and capping of welfare benefits for a new baby conceived or born while a mother was receiving welfare. After the passage of the 1996 welfare reform law, many states adopted these and many other approaches first tried under welfare waivers.

In addition, a number of other policy interventions are generally thought to have promoted work compared to welfare over the period examined in this chapter. Expanded eligibility and funding for child care has helped made work possible for mothers who otherwise might have difficulty finding child care. For example, the 1988 Family Support Act expanded eligibility for child care assistance in the form of transitional child care assistance for families working their way off AFDC. In 1990, federally funded child care assistance was extended to low-income families deemed to be at risk of receiving welfare under the Child Care and Development Block Grant (CCDBG).[3] Expansions to the Earned Income Tax Credit (EITC) in 1990 (phased-in 1991 and 1992) and in 1993 (phased-in 1994 through 1996) expanded the credit's "work bonus" to families with children, amounting to as much as 40 cents on each dollar earned for a low-income

---

[1] See for example, CRS Report 93-7, *Demographic Trends Affecting Aid to Families with Dependent Children (AFDC) Caseload Growth,* by Thomas Gabe; and, Peskin, Janice. Forecasting AFDC Caseloads, with an Emphasis on Economic Factors. Congressional Budget Office Staff Memorandum, July 1993.

[2] Section 1115 of the Social Security Act grants the Secretary authority to waive compliance of states with certain sections of the Social Security Act for state experiments or demonstrations which the Secretary judges to promote specific objectives of the Act.

[3] See: CRS Report 96-780, *Child Care for Low-Income Families: Federal Programs and Welfare Reform,* by Karen Spar.

family with two children.[4] Over the period examined in this chapter, the minimum wage was increased 4 times.[5] Additionally, most states allowed inflation to substantially erode the real value of welfare benefits over this period, diminishing the value of welfare relative to work.[6] Furthermore, since the passage of TANF, most states have increased financial work incentives for families receiving cash assistance by allowing families to keep more of their cash welfare benefit as their earnings increase.[7]

Untangling the effects of demographic factors, the economy, welfare policy and other policy interventions on single-mothers' work behavior, welfare receipt, income, and poverty status, is beyond the scope of this chapter. Others have attempted to parcel out these effects with mixed success and differing conclusions as to the relative impacts of each.[8] In contrast to these efforts, this chapter is intended to simply describe changes in single mothers' welfare, work, income and poverty status that have occurred over the past 13 years. The analysis which follows relies on data from the U.S. Bureau of the Census March CPS data. Over the period examined, the March CPS data provides a comparatively consistent approach for assessing changes in the economic status of single-mothers and their families. The March CPS asks questions about family composition in March, family members' labor force and employment status in the month, and retrospective accounting of income and labor force participation during the prior year. The data presented in this section capture family composition from March 1988 to March

---

[4] For a description of the EITC, see: CRS Report RS20470, *The Earned Income Tax Credit: Current Issues and Benefit Amounts,* by Melinda Gish. For an analysis of the possible effects of the EITC on welfare receipt and mothers' work, see: Meyer, Brace D., and Dan T. Rosenbaum. Welfare, the Earned Income Tax Credit, and the Labor Supply of Single Mothers. NBER Working Paper No. 7363, September 1999 (hereafter cited as Meyer and Rosenbaum. Welfare, the Earned Income Tax Credit).

[5] The federal minimum wage increased from $3.35 per hour to $3.80 per hour, effective April 1990, to $4.25 per hour, effective April 1991, to $4.75 per hour, effective October 1996, and $5.15 per hour, effective September 1997. For an analysis of possible effects of minimum wage increases on welfare participation, see: Turner, Mark. The Effects of Minimum Wages on Welfare Recipiency. Paper presented at the National Association for Welfare Research and Statistics, August 1998.

[6] Maximum TANF benefits available for a family of three in the median state in January 2000 were nearly 22% below the maximum level available to a family under AFDC in January 1987, after adjusting for the effects of price inflation. In only one state, Hawaii, were TANF benefits in January 2000 equal to the January 1987 AFDC benefit level, and in one state, New Mexico, higher, after adjusting for price inflation. In all other states, maximum price adjusted TANF benefits were lower in January 2000 than January 1987 AFDC benefits.

[7] For a discussion of changes in work incentives under TANF compared to AFDC see; CRS Report (forthcoming), *Changes to Earnings Disregards Under the TANF (Temporary Assistance for Needy Families) Program and their Affect on Eligibility and Benefits,* by Craig Abbey.

[8] See, for example: Council of Economic Advisors. Technical Report: "Explaining the Decline in Welfare Receipt, 1993-1996." A Report by the Council of Economic Advisers, Washington, D.C. April 1997; Ziliak, James P., Figlio, David N., Davis, Elizabeth E., and Connolly, Laura S. "Accounting for the Decline in AFDC Caseloads, Welfare Reform or the Economy?" The Journal of Human Resources, vol. XXXV, no, 3, p. 570-586. Moffitt, Robert A. The Effect of Pre-PRWORA Waivers on AFDC Caseloads and Female Earnings, Income, and Labor Force Behavior, in Economic Conditions and Welfare Reform. Danziger, Sheldon (ed.), Kalamazoo, Mich. W.E. Upjohn Institute for Employment Research, 1999.

2000, and family income and poverty status from 1987 to 1999, for a representative cross-section of families headed by single mothers in each year.[9]

---

[9] Unlike longitudinal surveys, the CPS does not follow the same families from year to year. Longitudinal surveys allow for the study of how individual families' circumstances change over time.

Chapter 2

OVERVIEW

CPS data show an increase in cash welfare receipt (AFDC, TANF, or other assistance) among single mothers during the late 1980s and early 1990s and a decrease in the mid-to-late 1990s. The CPS data generally correspond to the caseload rise and fall documented by administrative program data, but underestimates the caseload statistics to some extent.[1] Figure 1 shows that the total number of single mothers increased from 8.4 million in 1989, to about 9.9 million in 1993, an increase of 1.5 million, or 17%. Since 1993, the number of single mothers has remained fairly stable, between 9.8 and 10 million, but the number of single mothers receiving cash welfare has fallen each year.

The number of single mothers in families reporting receipt of cash welfare on the CPS increased from 2.5 million in 1989, to 3.4 million in 1993, an increase of 900,000, or 36% over the 4-year period. Since 1993, the number of single mothers reporting cash welfare has fallen to 1.5 million in 1999, (a 55% decline) (the bottom-shaded portion in Figure 1).[2] Over the same period, the number of poor single mothers who reported receiving no cash welfare increased by 495,000, from 1.721 million in 1993 to 2.216 million in 1999 (the middle-shaded area in Figure 1).

Figure 2 provides an overview of single mothers' welfare, work and poverty status from 1987 to 1999. The figure shows that since 1993, the share of single mothers who worked at some time during the year has increased markedly and that the share who received cash welfare (AFDC and, post-1996 TANF) has declined significantly, as has the share who are poor under the official poverty definition.[3]

---

[1] See Appendix A, which compares CPS estimates to AFDC/TANF caseload counts.
[2] Administrative caseload statistics show the caseload as peaking in March 1994, with nearly 5.1 million cases. By December 1999, the caseload had dropped to under 2.4 million cases; nearly a 54% decline from its March 1994 peak.
[3] The "official" U.S. Census Bureau definition counts cash, pre-tax, income against poverty thresholds that vary by family size and composition, in 1999, for example, a single mother with one child would be considered poor if her income were below $ 11,483, and if she had two children, below $13,423.

Figure 1. Single Mothers: Poverty and Cash Welfare Receipt, 1987 to 1999

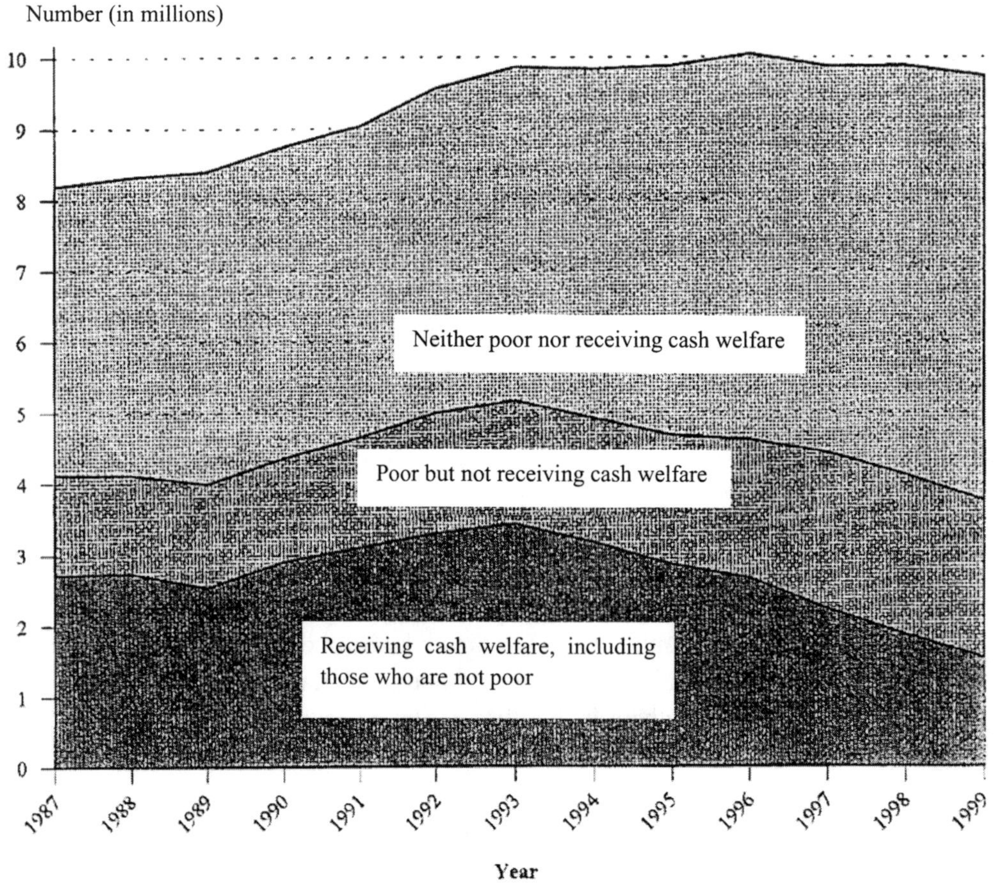

Number (in millions)

[Stacked area chart showing three categories from 1987 to 1999: "Neither poor nor receiving cash welfare", "Poor but not receiving cash welfare", and "Receiving cash welfare, including those who are not poor"]

Year

Source: Prepared by the Congressional Research Service (CRS). Based on Analysis of U.S. Census Bureau March 1988 to 2000 Current Population Survey (CPS) data.

Figure 2 shows that during the 1987 to 1993 period, the share of single mothers who worked at any time during the year hovered just below 70% in most years; since 1993, the share working has increased each year, reaching 82% in 1999. During the 1987 to 1993 period, roughly one-out-of-three single mothers received cash welfare. In 1993, the most recent peak year of welfare receipt on the CPS, about 35% of single mothers received cash welfare; since then the cash welfare receipt rate has declined each year, falling to just below 16% in 1999 – less than half the 1993 rate. The figure shows that the poverty rate among single mothers which from 1987 to 1993 ranged from 44% to 45% (except in 1989), has fallen from about 45% in 1993 to 34% in 1999.

Figure 2. Welfare, Work and Poverty Status Among Single Mothers, 1987 to 1999

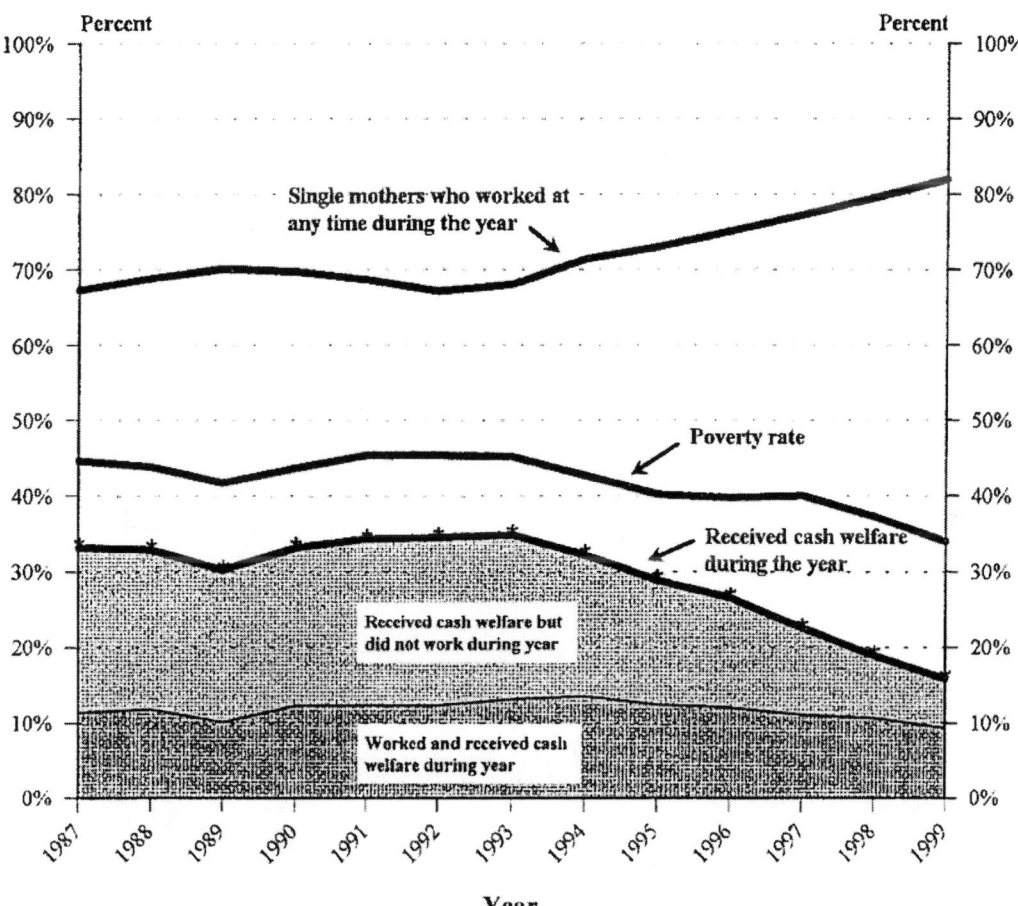

Source: Prepared by the Congressional Research Service (CRS). Based on Analysis of U.S. Census Bureau March 1988 to 2000 Current Population Survey (CPS) data.

Chapter 3

SINGLE MOTHERS' EMPLOYMENT RATES

While welfare receipt has declined, dramatic gains in single mothers' employment have occurred since 1993. Figure 3 shows employment rates of single and married mothers by age of youngest child in March, from 1988 to 2000. The chart shows that gaps that had existed between single and married mothers' employment have virtually been eliminated in recent years, with single mothers now being more likely than their married counterparts to be working.

The increase in employment among single mothers with young children has been most dramatic. Among mothers with a child under the age of 3, their employment rate increased from a recent low of 35.1% in March 1993 to a high of 59.1% in March 2000, a 24 percentage point increase over the period. Single mothers with a youngest child age 3-5 also experienced marked employment gains over the mid-to-late 1990s. Their employment rate grew from a recent low of 54.1% in March 1992, to 72.7% by March 2000, an 18.6 percentage point increase over the period. In March 2000, the employment rate of single mothers with a youngest child age 3-5 surpassed that of their married counterparts by 6.7 percentage points. Single mothers whose youngest child was of school age (age 6-17) had employment rates about equal to those of their married counterparts over the 1988-2000 period.

The healthy economy, combined with a transformed welfare system, improvements to the EITC, and increases in the minimum wage, are among factors thought to have encouraged work among single mothers in recent years. TANF, and the AFDC waivers that preceded it, transformed cash assistance from a needs-based entitlement to a program of temporary assistance, encouraging work and personal responsibility. Imposition of work requirements, time limits, and sanctions, and in most states, more generous earnings disregards, all serve to encourage work, either in lieu of welfare, or for a temporary period, in conjunction with welfare. The EITC, which is conditioned on earnings, is thought to encourage work among most groups, especially single parents who were not working, or who were marginally attached to the labor market. Increases in the EITC, passed by Congress in 1993 and phased in between 1994 and 1996, have increased the financial incentive for single mothers to work.[1] Other factors, such as increased funding for child care subsidies, may also have contributed to making work possible for more single mothers.

Figure 3. Employment Rates of Single Mothers and Married Mothers by Age of Youngest Child, March 1988 to March 2000

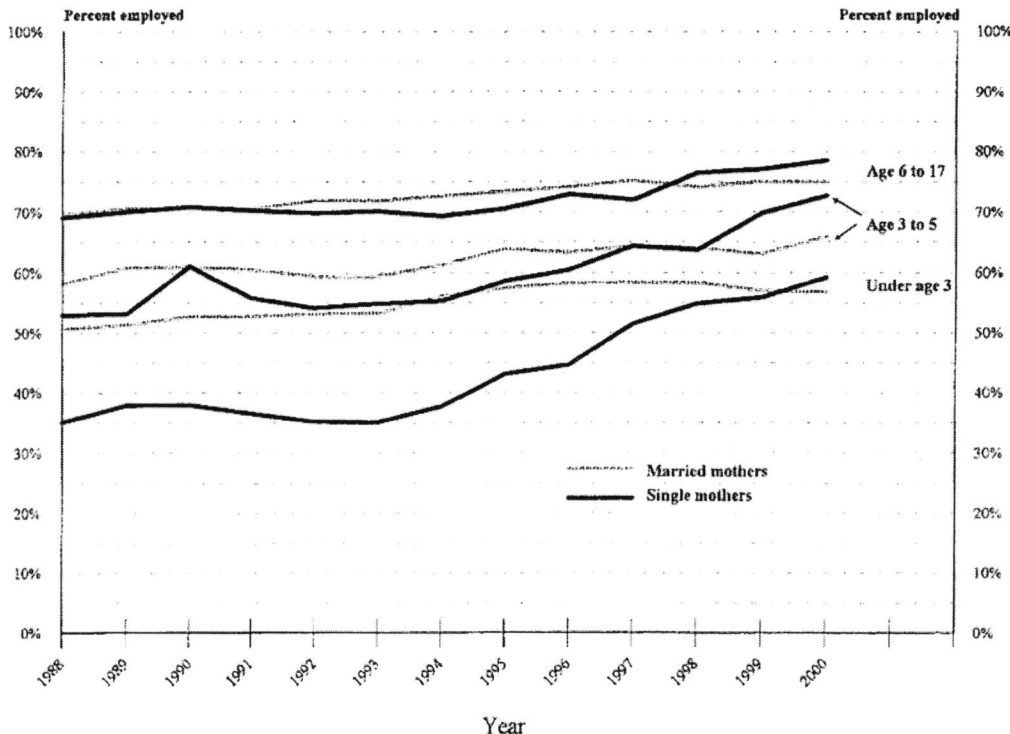

Source: Prepared by the Congressional Research Service (CRS). Based on analysis of U.S. Census Bureau March 1988 to 2000 Current Population Survey (CPS) data.

---

[1] Meyer and Rosenbaum, (Hereafter cited as Meyer and Rosenbaum. Welfare, the Earned Income Tax Credit), attribute 60% of the increase in single mothers weekly and annual employment between 1984 and 1996 to the EITC.

Chapter 4

WELFARE RECEIPT AMONG SINGLE MOTHERS

Figure 4 shows that cash welfare recipiency rates among single mothers overall, and among *poor* single mothers based on their pre-transfer income (i.e., cash income excluding cash welfare), remained fairly steady during the 1987-93 period, but have fallen considerably since. Among single mothers overall, about one-third received cash welfare during the late-1980s and early 1990s, with a low of about 30% in 1989 and a peak of about 35% in 1993. Cash welfare recipiency rates among single mothers began to fall after 1993, falling to just below 16% in 1999 – less than half the rate of 6 years earlier.

Recent declines in cash welfare recipiency rates have not simply been due to diminished need for assistance, as recipiency rates have fallen even among mothers who would appear to be in economic need, based on their pre-transfer income relative to poverty. For example, Figure 4 shows that among single mothers who were poor based on their pre-transfer cash income, the share who received cash welfare generally hovered around 63% over the 1987-93 period. Since 1993, the cash welfare recipiency rate among single mothers with pre-transfer income below poverty has fallen each year, reaching a low of 36% in 1999.

Figure 5 shows cash welfare recipiency rates in greater detail by families' level of financial need, as measured by families' levels of pre-transfer income relative to poverty. The figure shows that cash welfare recipiency rates have fallen considerably in recent years even among single mothers who might be considered especially needy by having very low levels of pre-transfer income relative to poverty. For example, the top line of Figure 5 shows that nearly 90% of single mothers with no pre-transfer income reported receiving cash assistance from 1987 to 1990. However, since 1990, the reported rate of cash welfare recipiency among this group drifted downwards, to 77% in 1996, and afterwards fell abruptly, to about 57% by 1999. Similarly, for single mothers with very low pre-transfer income relative to poverty (below 25% of poverty), and for families with pre-transfer incomes between 25 and 50% of poverty, cash welfare recipiency rates also show dramatic declines after 1996: for the former group from 72% in 1996 to 46% in 1999, and for the latter group from 60% in 1995 to 38% in 1999.

Figure 4. Single Mothers: Cash Welfare Recipiency Rates, 1987 to 1999

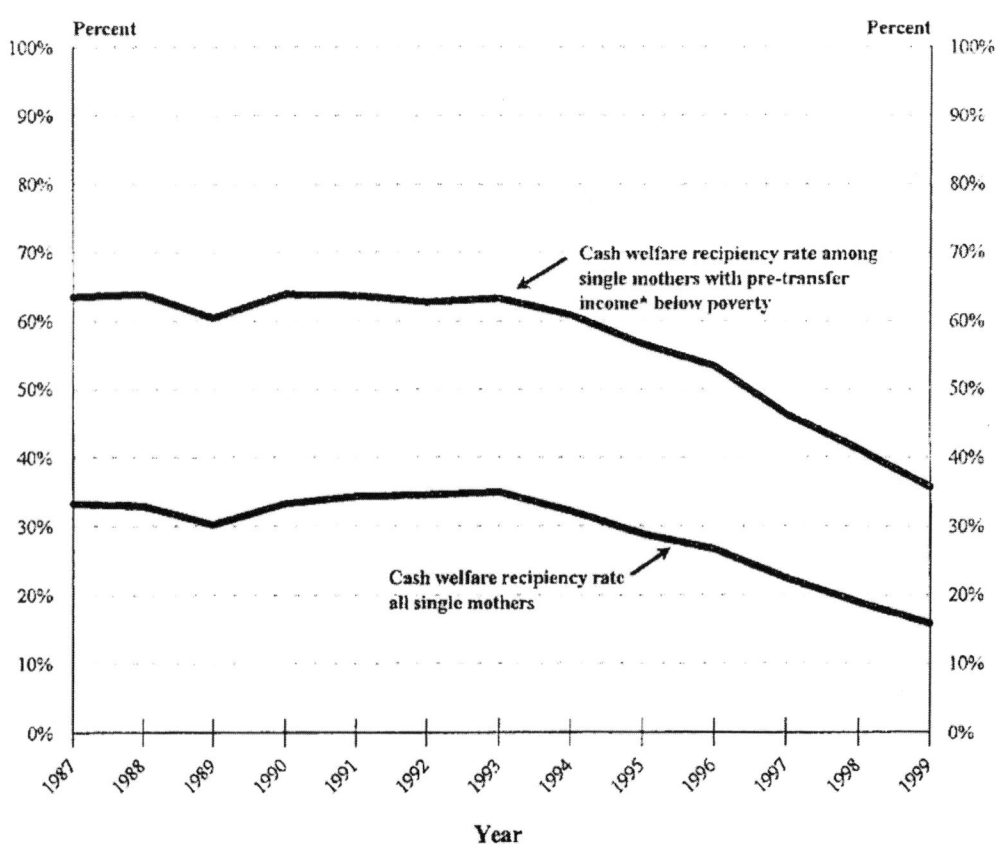

Source: Prepared by the Congressional Research Service (CRS). Based on analysis of U.S. Census Bureau March 1988 to 2000 Current Population Survey (CPS) data.
* Pre-transfer income is cash income other than cash welfare payments.

Likewise, food stamp recipiency rates among low-income households have also fallen in recent years, although the declines have not been as dramatic as the declines in cash welfare recipiency rates shown above. Figure 6 shows that in 1994, 71% of single-mother families with household income below 130% of poverty (the Food Stamp Program's gross income qualifying limit) reported receiving food stamp benefits; by 1999 the share had fallen to about 51%. Among those with household incomes below 50% of the low-household income threshold, in 1994, 80% reported food stamp receipt; in 1999 just 63% reported food stamp receipt.

To at least some extent, the declining cash welfare and food stamp recipiency rates shown in Figures 4 through 6 are likely due to increased underreporting of welfare receipt on the CPS. Worsened reporting of cash welfare on the CPS makes it difficult to gauge how much of the drop in welfare receipt among female-headed families with children represents eligible families who do not receive assistance rather than families who do not report actual welfare aid on the CPS. See Appendix A for an analysis of the possible extent of under-reporting of cash welfare on the CPS.

Figure 5. Cash Welfare Recipiency Rates Among Single Mother Families by Pre-transfer Income* Poverty Status, 1987 to 1999

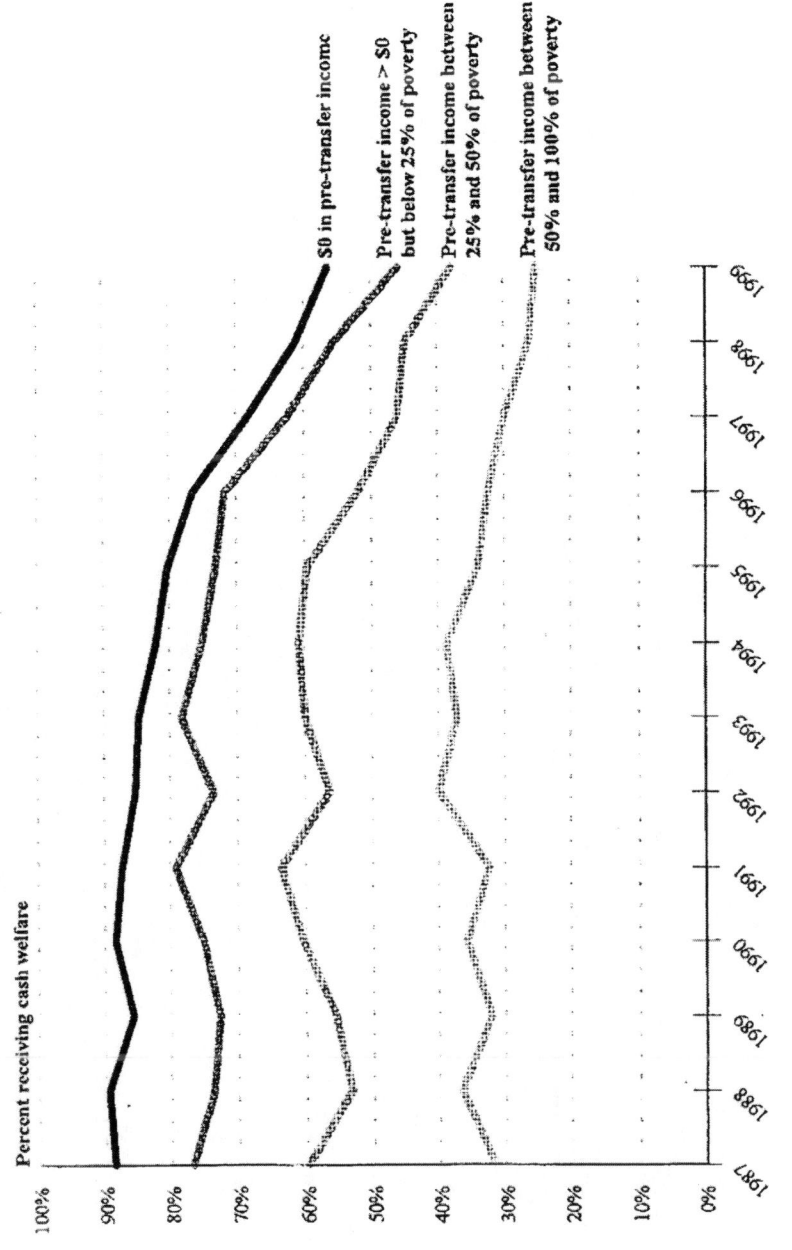

Source: Prepared by the Congressional Research Service (CRS). Based on analysis of U.S. Census Bureau March 1988 to 2000 Current Population Survey (CPS) data.

* Cash income excluding cash welfare relative to poverty.

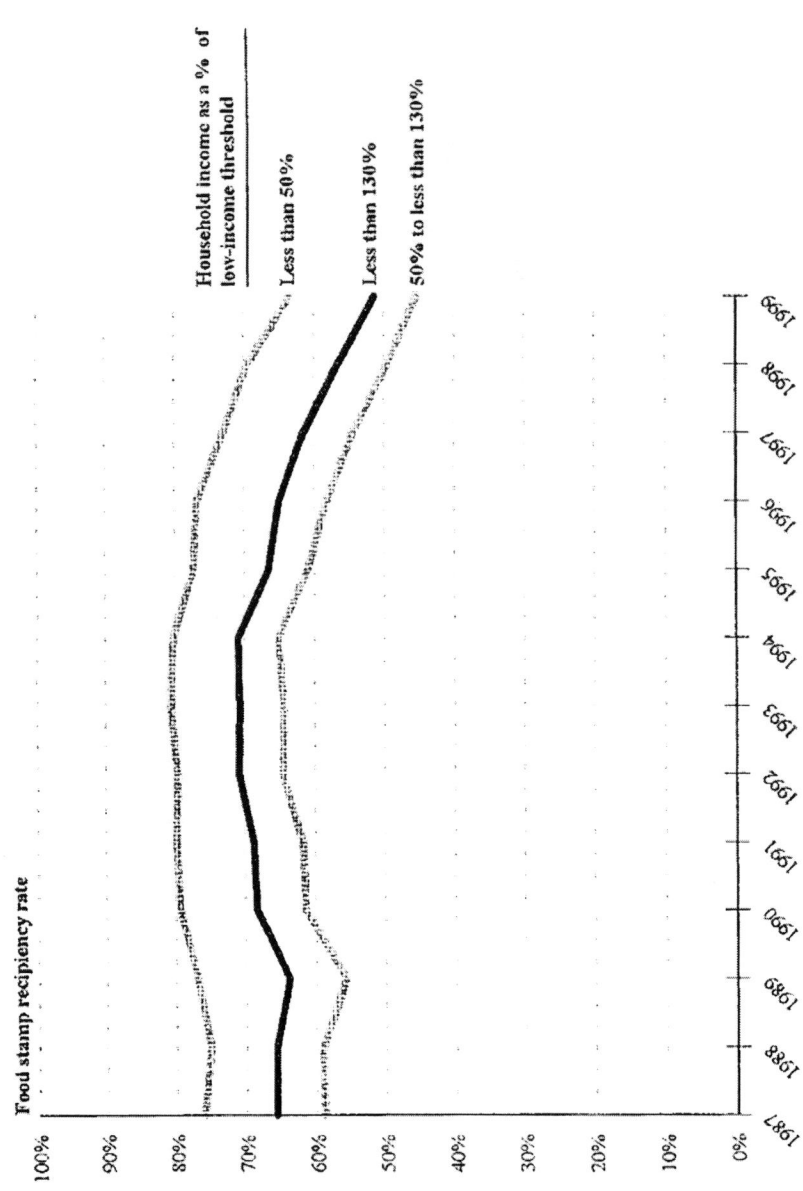

Figure 6. Food Stamp Recipiency Rates among Single Mothers, by Household Income Relative to Household Low-Income Threshold 1987 to 1999

Source: Prepared by the Congressional Research Service (CRS). Based on analysis of U.S. Census Bureau March 1988 to 2000 Current Population Survey (CPS) data.

Chapter 5

POOR SINGLE MOTHERS' WORK AND WELFARE STATUS

Although poverty rates among single mothers have declined in recent years, there is a greater likelihood today, than in years past that a *poor* single mother will be working, rather than receiving welfare. As shown above, poor single mothers are less likely to be receiving cash welfare in recent than in earlier years (Figures 4 and 5). Similarly, like all single mothers, *poor* single mothers are also now more likely to be working than not. Changes in poor mothers' participation in work and welfare status first became evident in the early-to-mid 1990s, with rates of employment increasing after 1992 and rates of welfare receipt declining after 1993 (see Figure 7, top 2 lines). A crossover point was reached between 1995 and 1996, when the chances that a *poor* single mother would be working exceeded the chances that she would be receiving welfare.

Figure 7 shows that the share *of poor* single mothers who received cash welfare at any time during the year fell from just over 60% in the 1987-93 period, to about 33% in 1999. The rate of decline in welfare receipt among *poor* single mothers has been greatest since 1996, a period coinciding with the passage and implementation of national welfare reform legislation. Similarly, the share of poor single mothers who were working at any time during the year increased from around 44% in 1992, to about 64% in 1999, regardless of whether they were receiving cash welfare.

The share *of poor* single mothers who relied on cash welfare without working dropped from a peak of 43% in 1991, to about 15% in 1999 (just over one-third the 1991 rate). The share of *poor* single mother who worked without relying on cash welfare has increased from a recent low of about 25% in 1993, to nearly 47% in 1999 (not quite double the 1993 rate). The share *of poor* single mothers who combined work and welfare over the year has remained relatively constant over the past 13 years, at around 20%.

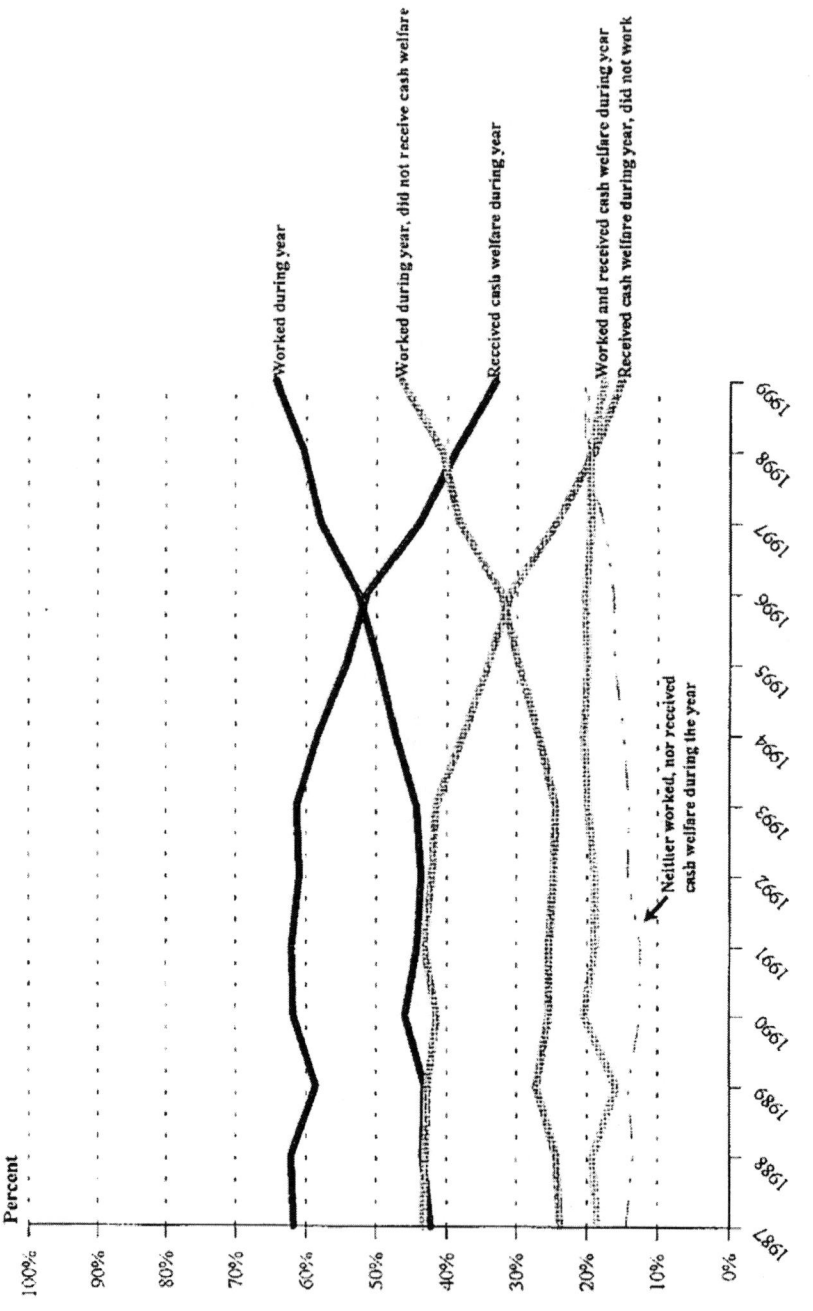

Figure 7. Poor Single Mothers: Work and Welfare Status During the Year 1987 to 1999

Source: Prepared by the Congressional Research Service (CRS). Based on analysis of U.S. Census Bureau March 1988 to 2000 Current Population Survey (CPS) data.

The share *of poor* single mothers who reported that they neither worked nor received cash welfare during the year (the dashed line in Figure 7) has increased from a low of about 12% in 1991 to around 20% in 1999. This surprising combination may reflect a mix of circumstances, including income or support from other sources such as family members, support from unrelated household members (which is not included in the official poverty measure), and other means of support from outside the household not captured on the CPS. It may also reflect income reporting problems on the CPS, especially with regard to welfare income.[1] Finally, welfare diversion and sanction policies may have contributed to the increased number of poor mothers neither working nor receiving welfare.

---

[1] See *Appendix A* on CPS under-reporting.

Chapter 6

EFFECTS OF EARNINGS, TRANSFERS, AND TAXES ON SINGLE MOTHERS' POVERTY STATUS

As shown earlier, in Figure 2, single mothers' poverty status has improved since 1993. Changes in the economy and changes in welfare policy and other programs, such as the EITC, have both direct and indirect effects on income and poverty. However, the official U.S. poverty measure counts only family cash income (excluding capital gains and lump sum or one-time payments) against a family's poverty threshold (which varies by family size and composition) to determine whether a family is counted as poor. The definition does not include the value of in-kind benefits, such as food stamps, school lunches, or public housing subsidies, nor does it include the effects of taxes or tax credits such as the EITC. Inclusion of in-kind benefits and the EITC provides a more comprehensive income definition than the official definition. Additionally, other unrelated household members may contribute to the family's economic well-being, but determining the extent to which resources are shared among unrelated household members is often difficult.

Figure 8 shows the effects of income from these other sources on poverty among all single mothers. Components of family income are sequentially added and measured against families' poverty thresholds, as one moves from the top line of the chart to subsequent lines below:

- **Line 1:** The top line shows the percent of single mothers who would be counted as poor if only family earnings were counted against the poverty line.
- **Line 2:** The second line down includes other sources of cash income, in addition to earnings, that were already counted above (e.g., social security payments, unemployment compensation, workers compensation, interest and dividends, inter-family transfers). However, this line does not include cash welfare.
- **Line 3:** The third line down adds cash welfare to the other sources already mentioned, and with those sources, represents the income definition used in the *official poverty measure*.

Lines 4 through 6 include food stamps, taxes (including the effects of the EITC) and income of other unrelated household members that are not included under the "official" U.S. Bureau of the Census poverty definition:

- **Line 4:** The fourth line down shows the market value of food stamps when added to cash income and compared to the family poverty threshold.
- **Line 5:** The fifth line down shows the effect of adding the value of the EITC, less federal and state income taxes and payroll taxes, to line 4.
- **Line 6:** The bottom (dashed) line shows the effects of counting all income in the household in which the single mother lives, not just that of her related family members, and comparing it to an unofficial "household low-income threshold." The household low-income threshold used here applies family poverty income thresholds, which are based on family size and composition, to households, based on household size and composition. It must be noted that official poverty measurement is based on a family concept, which assumes that family members share income and economies of scale that result from shared living arrangements. It is generally agreed among researchers that assumptions regarding income sharing and shared economies of scale among related family members, who have ties based on blood, marriage, and adoption, do not apply to the same extent among unrelated household members. Consequently, these estimates of household low-income status likely overstate the effect of household income on reducing poverty among families headed by single mothers.

In viewing Figure 8, note that the trend in earnings is the principal factor affecting the declining trend in poverty, whereas the other income sources, with the exception of the EITC, affect the level of poverty, more than its trend over time. Evidence of this effect is that most lines in the chart, with the exception of the EITC, roughly run parallel to the ones above.

EFFECT OF EARNINGS AND OTHER NONWELFARE CASH INCOME ON POVERTY

Figure 8 shows that between 1993 and 1999, single mothers' poverty, based on family earnings alone, fell from 56.2% to 43.6% (line 1). Adding other cash income, except cash welfare, to family earnings (line 2), reduces poverty in 1993 from 56.2% to 47.4, and in 1999 from 43.6% to 35.3%.

Figure 8. Effects of Earnings, Transfers and Taxes on Family Poverty and Household Low-Income Status of Single Mothers, 1987 to 1999

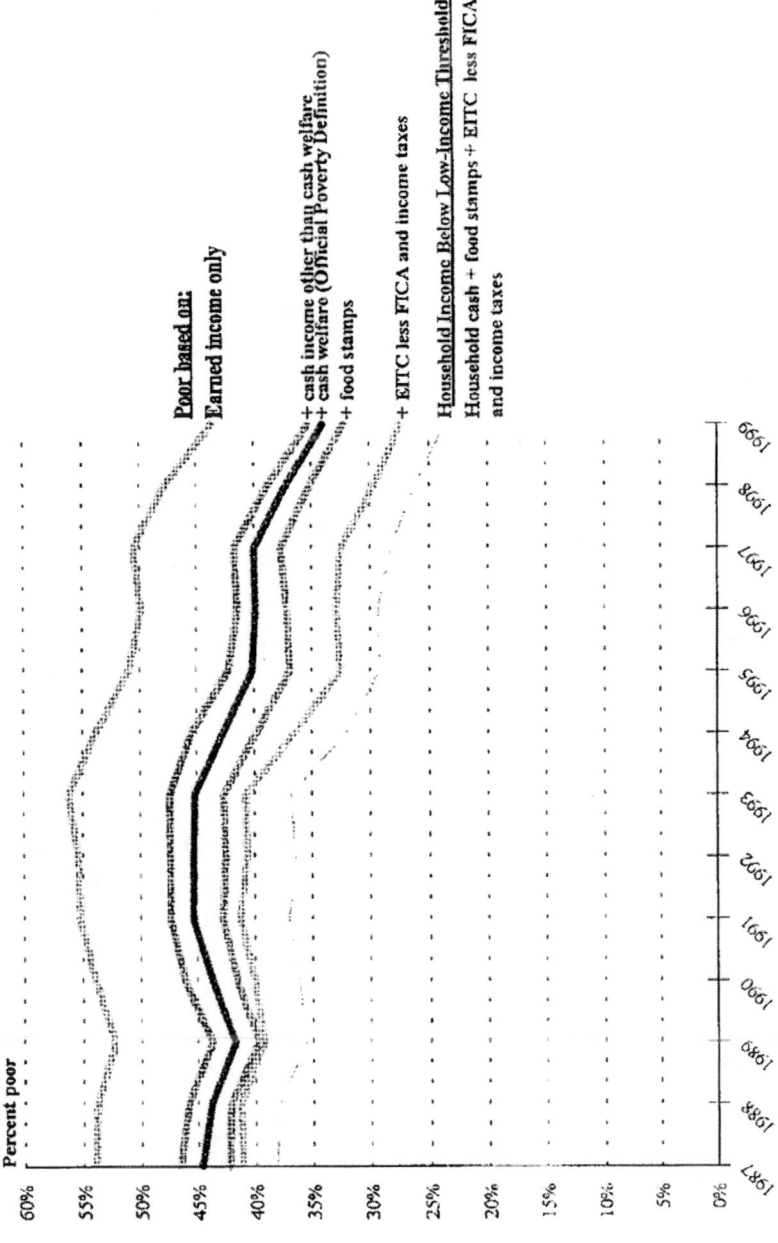

Source: Prepared by the Congressional Research Service (CRS). Based on analysis of U.S. Census Bureau March 1988 to 2000 Current Population Survey (CPS) data.

EFFECT OF CASH WELFARE ON POVERTY

When added to other income, cash welfare benefits have only a small impact on the poverty rate, as these benefits generally are not sufficient, even when combined with other cash income, to lift families above the federal poverty threshold. In the vast majority of states the level of earnings or other cash income at which states' cash welfare benefits under TANF become unavailable for a family are well below the poverty line for example. In January 2000, in only 10 states could a single mother with two children have earnings above the poverty line and still continue to receive TANF cash assistance.[1] Consequently, cash welfare benefits have little impact on the poverty rate. The addition of cash welfare (line 3, representing the official income definition for measuring poverty) reduces poverty only slightly: from 47.4% (line 2) to 45.2% (line 3) in 1993, and from 35.3% to 34.0% in 1999. Nonetheless, cash welfare benefits can have a significant impact on the level of poor families' incomes, affecting the degree to which their incomes fall below the poverty income standard. This impact is not captured by changes in the poverty rate as shown in Figure 8.

THE EFFECT ON POVERTY OF COUNTING SELECTED INCOME SOURCES NOT INCLUDED IN THE "OFFICIAL" POVERTY MEASURE

The following three measures include income from sources not included under the "official" U.S. Bureau of the Census poverty definition (i.e., food stamps, taxes (including the effects of the EITC) and income of other unrelated household members.

Effect of Food Stamps on Poverty

The fourth line from the top in Figure 8 shows the effect on the poverty rate of single mothers by counting the value of food Stamps. The line shows that food stamps reduce the poverty rate of single mothers from about 2 to 3 percentage points over the period. The anti-poverty effectiveness of food stamps seems to have lessened somewhat in recent years. In 1995, food stamps reduced the poverty rate from 40.2% (its official measure) to 36.9%, a 3.3 percentage point (8.1%) reduction in poverty. In 1999, food stamps reduced the poverty rate from its official rate of 34.0%, to 32.2%, a 1.8 percentage point (5.3%) reduction.

---

[1] See U.S. House of Representatives Committee on Ways and Means. *2000 Green Book*. Table 7-13 (Breakeven Points), pp. 398-400. Washington, D.C. Oct. 6, 2000.

Effect of the EITC and Taxes on Poverty

As noted above, the net effect of the EITC[2] (after counting the effect of reductions in income from federal and state income taxes and FICA taxes) (line 5), when added to total family cash income and food stamps (line 4), causes a divergence in trend from the lines above. This is especially notable after 1993. A major expansion of the EITC, passed by Congress in 1993 and phased in between 1994 and 1996, increased the amount of the EITC work bonus families might receive. The anti-poverty effectiveness of the EITC was approximately three times greater in 1999 than in 1993. In 1993, the EITC reduced the poverty rate (counting food stamps) among single mothers from 42.7% (line 4), to 40.7% (line 5), a 2.0 percentage point (4.6%) reduction. In 1999, the EITC reduced poverty from 32.2% to 29.7%, a 4.7 percentage point (14.6%) reduction.

As receipt of the EITC is conditioned on earnings, the growing impact of the EITC in part reflects the rise in work rates among single mothers. Among those who are working and poor (before counting the EITC), the EITC helps lift the income of some above the poverty line. Although the EITC expansion provided additional income to low-income families who were already working, it may also have helped induce increased employment among family heads with low to moderate earnings potential, and thus contributed to the decline in poverty based on earned income only that has occurred since 1993 (shown as the top line in the chart).

Note too, that to the extent that changes in cash welfare programs in recent years have encouraged work (such as work requirements and increased earnings disregards), these changes may have had an indirect effect on poverty by increasing earnings and, through earnings, making the EITC available to a greater number of families.

Effect of Unrelated Household Member's Income on Poverty

The household low-income line (bottom line) shows that if all household members' income were shared equally among household members, the poverty rate among single mothers would drop by at most 3 to 4 percentage points over the 1987 to 1999 period. Adding other non-family members' income, and counting them as though they were family members who shared income equally, reduced the post in-kind transfer, post-tax, poverty rate in 1993 from 40.7% to 36.8%; in 1998 the post-in-kind transfer, post-tax, poverty rate would have dropped from 27.5% to 23.6%. Again, this is most likely an overstatement of the possible effect that shared household living arrangements might

---

[2] Note that the value of the EITC on the CPS is based on Census Bureau imputations, rather than actual reported tax credits. Also, the EITC is different from most sources of income, as most families receive the EITC as a lump sum refund.

have on single mothers' poverty status, because of uncertainty about the extent to which such income is actually shared.

Chapter 7

DEGREE OF POVERTY AMONG POOR SINGLE MOTHERS

As noted above, the poverty rate measures only the percent of families whose incomes fall below their respective poverty thresholds, based on family size and composition. Although the poverty rate provides an overall indication of the level of need in the population, it does not measure the extent of need among poor families. Figure 9 and 10 show two different measures of the *"poverty gap"* among poor families headed by single mothers – that is, the degree to which poor families incomes fall below the poverty income level. In these figures the poverty gap is depicted as family income as a percent of poverty among poor families. Figure 9 is based on the cash income poverty measure, whereas figure 10 is based on cash income plus the value of food assistance and taxes (including the EITC). Note that the families depicted in figure 10 are a subset of those included in figure 9, as they are families who remain poor after considering food stamps and taxes (including the EITC) – the effects of which are not counted in figure 9. In each figure the extent of poverty among poor families is depicted at various percentiles, based on families' ranked by family income as a percent of poverty.

Figures 9 and 10 show that the median family income as a percent of need (i.e., poverty) among poor families has remained relatively steady over the past 13 years. Based on "official" cash income, for purposes of measuring poverty, the median family income as a percent of need among poor families headed by single mothers has ranged from a low of 48%, in 1988 and 1992, to as high as 53% of poverty in 1995 and 1999 (Figure 9). Looking at just the subset of single-mother families who were poor based on a more comprehensive income definition that includes food stamps and taxes (including the EITC), the median family income as a percent of need was somewhat higher over the period, ranging from a high of 65% of poverty, as recently as 1995, to a low of 62% of poverty, in 1998 and 1999 (Figure 10).

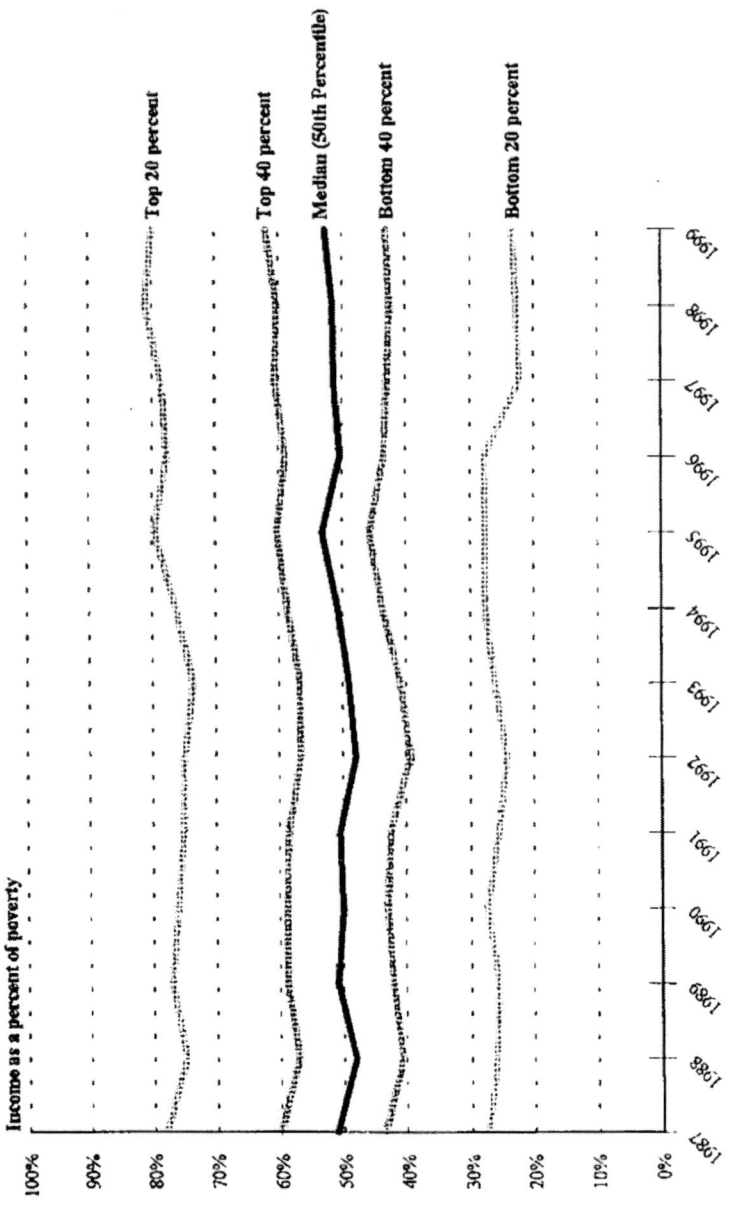

Figure 9. Poverty Gap* Percentiles Based on Cash Income for Poor Single-Mother Families, 1987 to 1999

Source: Prepared by the Congressional Research Service (CRS). Based on analysis of U.S. Census Bureau March 1988 to 2000 Current Population Survey (CPS) data.

* Poor families' cash income as a percent of families' poverty thresholds.

Figure 10. Poverty Gap* Percentiles Based on Net After-Tax Cash Income (including the EITC) and the Value of Food Stamps, for Poor Single-Mother Families, 1987 to 1999

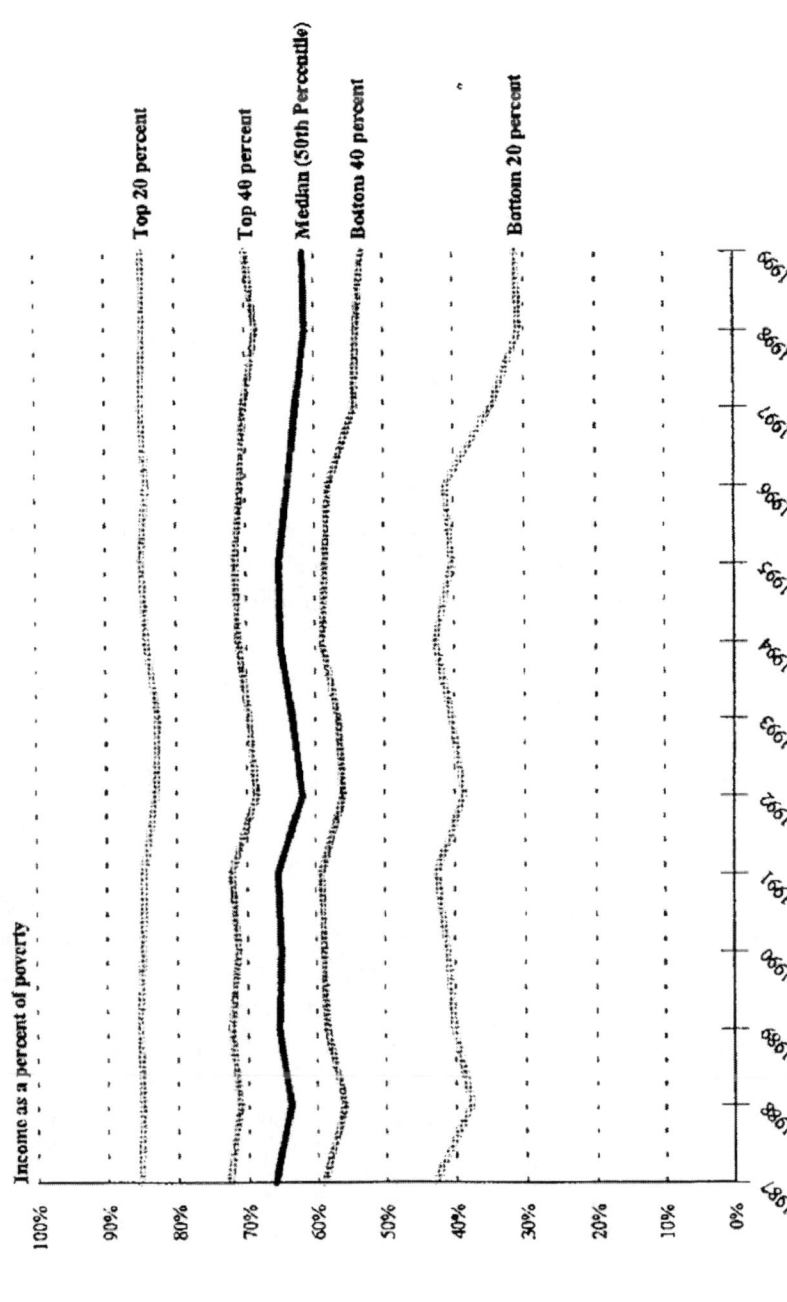

Source: Prepared by the Congressional Research Service (CRS). Based on analysis of US. Census Bureau March 1988 to 2000 Current Population Survey (CPS) date.

* Poor families' based on cash after-tax income and the market value of food stamps as a percent of families' poverty thresholds.

Both figures 9 and 10 show recent declines in income relative to poverty for the poorest families headed by single mothers. For example, figure 9, shows that the bottom 5th of poor single mothers, family income relative to poverty has fallen from a recent high of 28% of poverty in 1995, to 23% of poverty in 1998 and 1999. Looking at the subset of single-mother families that were poor based on the more comprehensive income definition (cash, food stamps, and taxes (including the EITC)), the bottom 5th have seen a decline in relative economic well-being from a high of 43% of poverty, in 1994, to a low of 31% of poverty in 1998 and 1999 (Figure 10).

SOURCES AND LEVEL OF INCOME AMONG LOWER-INCOME SINGLE MOTHERS

The composition and level of income among the single-mother families at the bottom of the income distribution has changed markedly in recent years, reflecting increased earnings supplemented by increased EITC and reductions in cash welfare and food stamps. For single mothers in the bottom fifth (bottom quintile), increased earnings and EITC have not been sufficient in recent years to offset losses in cash welfare and food stamps, resulting in reduced net income since 1994, the latest income peak for this group. Families in the bottom 20% to 40% (second quintile) also received less cash welfare and food stamps in recent years, but in 1999, increased earnings and EITC were sufficient to offset these losses.

Figures 11 and 12 examine sources of income among the bottom quintile (bottom 20%) and the second lowest quintile (bottom 20% to 40%) of single-mother families, respectively, based on their pre-tax cash income relative to poverty. The income to poverty ratios demarcating the break points at which a family qualifies as being in the bottom and second from the bottom quintiles are shown in Appendix B. The charts show the average annual income, in 1999 dollars, from the following sources: cash public assistance (AFDC, TANF, and General Assistance (GA)); Supplemental Security Income (SSI); food stamps (market value); child support and alimony; other cash income other than earnings; net earnings (earnings net of the employee share of FICA payroll taxes and any federal or state income taxes); and the EITC. The employee share of FICA payroll taxes, and any federal or state income tax payments are also shown as negative values. Note that these estimates are based on year-to-year income comparisons of cross-sectional survey data, rather than a comparison of incomes for the same families over time.

Figure 11 shows an upsurge in annual average income among single mothers in the bottom quintile, from 1993 to 1994. Average total income increased from $6,254 to $7,151; an increase of $897, or 14%. Components of the increase were: cash public assistance, $100 (4%); food stamps, $263 (12%); SSI, $86 (56%); net earnings, $323 (50%); and EITC, $156 (131%).

From 1994 through 1996, average total income among the bottom quintile of single-mother families remained essentially unchanged, drifting down slightly perhaps, despite dramatic changes in its composition. In 1995 and 1996, earnings of single mothers in the bottom quintile continued to increase, as did EITC, while cash assistance (AFDC and GA) and food stamps fell. The growing importance of the EITC as an earnings supplement over the 1994 to 1996 period can be illustrated by examining the average EITC as a share of average earnings. From 1993 to 1996, the EITC "work bonus" had doubled, from 18% to 37% of earnings.

Figure 11 further shows that average cash welfare and food stamp benefits reported by single mothers in the bottom quintile continued to decline during the 1997-1999 period, and that earnings combined with the EITC did not rise enough to offset this loss. As a result, average total family income for this population was lower in 1997-1999 than in 1994-1996; however, in 1999 was higher than in all years preceding 1994. Average annual cash welfare assistance received by single mothers in the bottom quintile in 1999 was 53% below what this group had received, on average, in the most recent peak year of 1994 ($1,184 versus $2,541). Food stamps, for this group in 1999 were 39% below their 1994 value ($1,509 versus $2,476). In contrast, net earnings in 1999 were over twice their 1994 level ($2,107 versus $988), and over 3-times their 1993 level ($2,107 versus $665). Nonetheless, while combined cash assistance and food stamps fell by $2,324 from 1994 to 1999, net earnings combined with EITC grew by $1,629, but offset only 70% of the loss in cash welfare and food stamps over the period.

Figure 12 is similar to Figure 11, but shows average income by source for the second quintile of single-mother families, ranked by their income relative to poverty. The chart shows comparatively large gains in average total income from 1993 to 1995, due largely to increased earnings and EITC. Over this period, average total net income increased from $11,468 to $14,752, a gain of nearly 27%. With the exception of 1996, average earnings for single mothers in the second quintile continued to grow; however, earnings and the EITC were insufficient to offset declines in cash assistance and food stamps in 1996 and 1997. From 1995 to 1997, combined earnings and EITC gains ($810) offset only 62% of the loss in combined cash assistance and food stamp benefits ($1,318) over the period.

By 1999, average total income among single mothers in the second quintile reached a new high. In 1999, earnings in combination with the EITC, were more than offsetting the loss in combined cash assistance and food stamps that occurred over the 1995 to 1999 period. Over the period, the gain in average net earnings, in combination with EITC ($3,817), more than offset the $2,521 loss in combined cash assistance and food stamps. By 1999, average net earnings accounted for well over half (56%) of these families' incomes ($8,770 in earnings out of a total net income of $15,679) and cash assistance ($906) accounted for just under 6%. In contrast, in 1987, earnings accounted for about 28% of this group's income ($3,437 in earnings out of a total net income of $12,278) and cash assistance ($4,249) comprised about 35%. In 1999, average total income for families in the second quintile ($15,679) was nearly 28% above that in 1987 ($12,278).

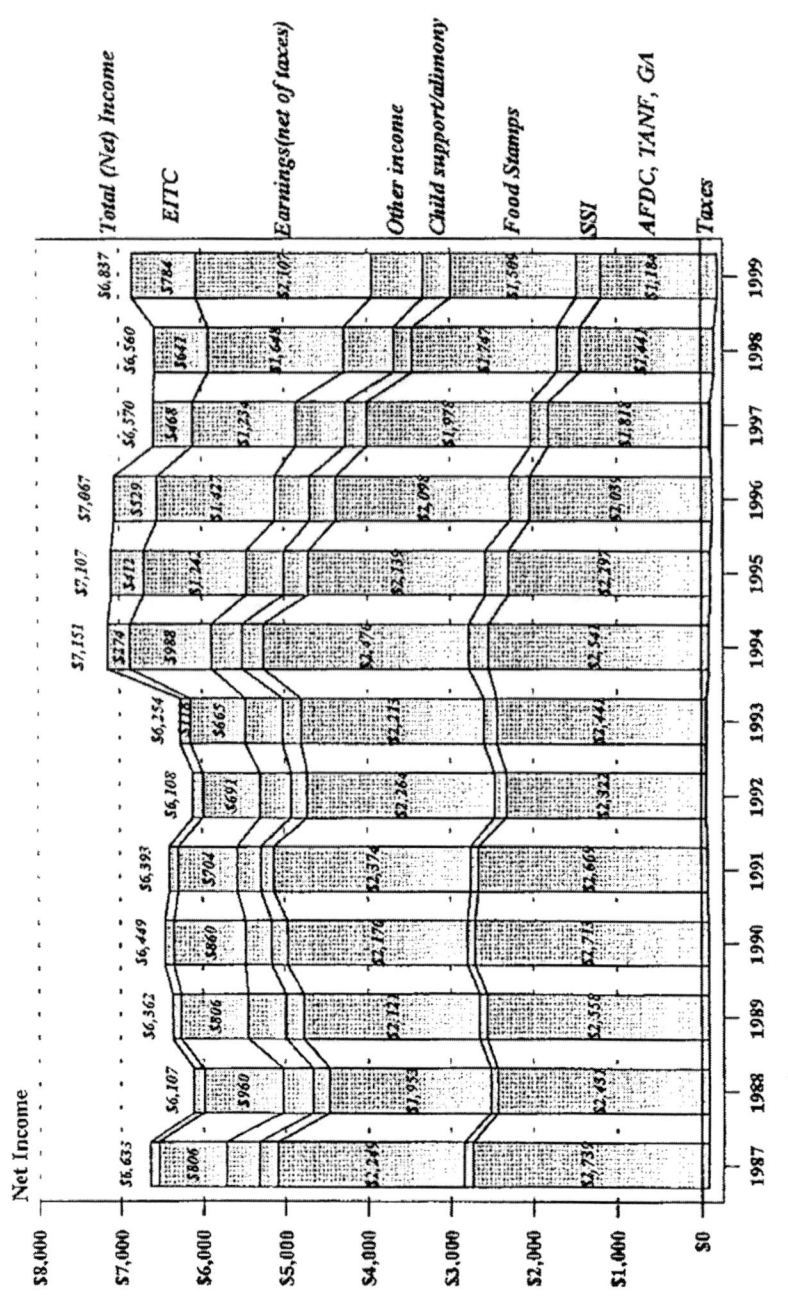

Figure 11. Bottom Quintile* of Single-Mother Families: Average Annual Income by Source, 1987 to 1999 (in 1999 dollars)

Source: Prepared by the Congressional Research Service (CRS). Based on analysis of U.S. Census Bureau March 1988 to 2000 Current Population Survey (CPS) data.

* Quintiles based on ranking of ratios of family cash, pre-tax income, relative to poverty. Taxes include federal and state income taxes and FICA taxes.

Figure 12. Second Quintile* of Single-Mother Families: Annual Average Income by Source, 1987 to 1999 (in 1999 dollars)

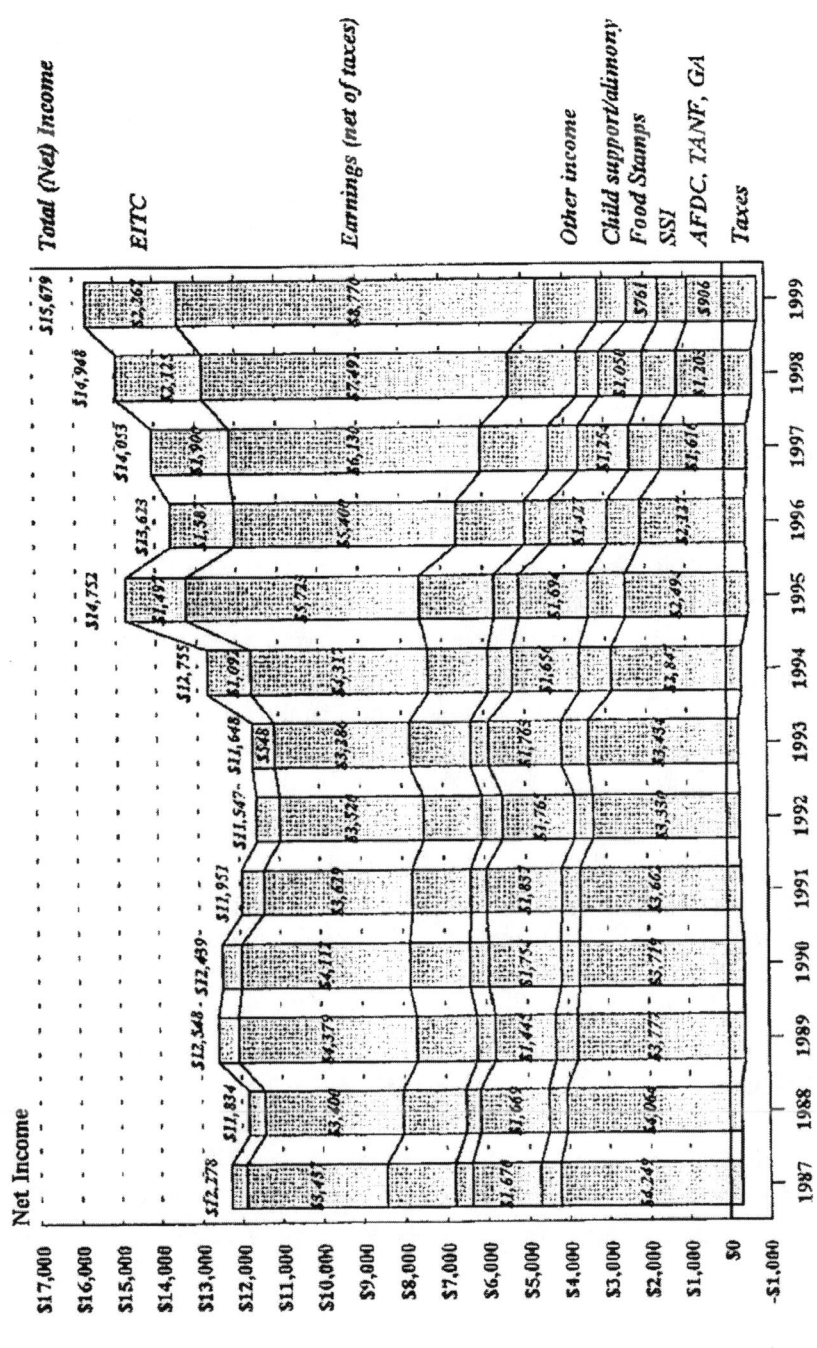

Source: Prepared by the Congressional Research Service (CRS). Based on analysis of U.S. Census Bureau March 1988 to 2000 Current Population Survey (CPS) data.

* Quintiles based on ranking of ratios of family cash, pre-tax income, relative to poverty. Taxes include federal and state income taxes and FICA taxes.

CONCLUSIONS AND POLICY IMPLICATIONS

CRS analysis of 13 years of U.S. Census Bureau CPS data shows a dramatic transformation in terms of welfare, work, and poverty status among single mothers over the period. CPS data generally follow the upsurge in the AFDC caseload evidenced by administrative/program statistics that occurred in the late-1980s and early 1990s, and the historic declines that followed. Increases in the number of families headed by single mothers during the late-1980s and early 1990s are likely to have contributed to the rapid growth in cash welfare caseloads under the AFDC program that occurred over the period. Since then the number of single mothers has remained relatively flat, at just under 10 million, and welfare caseloads have fallen dramatically. Economic conditions certainly contributed to the welfare caseload increase that began in the late 1980s, and the historic declines in the caseload that have occurred since their most recent peak in March 1994. A number of policy interventions have helped to increase the economic returns to work and to encourage work over welfare. Increases to the EITC and the minimum wage, and erosion of most states' welfare benefit levels due to inflation, have helped to increase the economic returns to work compared to welfare in recent years. States' extension of work requirements to mothers with younger children, increased welfare sanction authority, and adoption of time-limits on welfare receipt, first experimented with under AFDC waiver authority, and now widely adopted by states under TANF, have helped to transform the welfare system from an entitlement program to a program that emphasizes self-support, primarily through work, and personal responsibility.

The CPS data shows that single mothers are considerably more likely to be working, and less likely to be poor or receiving welfare in most recent than in earlier years (Figure 2). Although many of these changes precede passage of the 1996 welfare law, reductions in welfare receipt have since been especially large. Since 1996, *poor* single mothers are more likely to work during the year than to receive welfare (Figure 7). However, reductions in poverty among single mothers have not been as large as the concurrent declines in cash welfare receipt and increased work among single mothers in recent years. Moreover, CPS data indicate that welfare receipt rates among very poor families based on their pre-transfer (i.e., other than welfare) income have dropped considerably in recent years (Figure 5). Among single-mother families whose incomes are lowest (the bottom 20% of single-mothers based on family income relative to poverty), income from earnings supplemented by the EITC has grown markedly since 1993 but has failed to offset losses in cash welfare benefits and food stamps (Figure 10). While single mothers are less dependent on welfare in most recent than in past years, increased work has not resulted in marked gains in net income for the bottom fifth of single mothers, ranked by family income relative to poverty.

The CPS data show that although welfare receipt and poverty among single mothers has declined in recent years, mothers receiving welfare are now more likely to be working, and *poor* mothers are now less likely to be receiving welfare and more likely to be working than in past years. Prospects of single mothers working their way off welfare and out of poverty hinge in large part on their finding full-time, stable employment at a sufficient wage.

CPS data show that most single mothers work full-time schedules (35 or more hours per week) when they work (see Figure 13). Among single mothers who combined welfare and work during the year, 65% worked full-time schedules; among working single mothers who were poor but did not receive welfare, nearly an equal share (62%) worked full-time schedules. However, poor mothers not receiving cash welfare were more likely to have worked full-year (50 to 52 weeks) (45%) than their counterparts who received cash welfare (28%).

One policy challenge to reduce poverty and welfare dependency among single mothers may be to assist mothers in moving to full-time, full-year work. However, full-time full-year work is likely necessary, but not sufficient, for some single mothers to have incomes above poverty and not rely on cash welfare. Nearly 20% of single mothers who combined work and welfare worked full-time, full-year and 30% of poor single mothers who did not receive welfare worked full-time full-year (see Figure 13). For these mothers, full-time attachment to a job was insufficient to move them off of welfare or out of poverty. Single mothers with incomes somewhat above poverty (100% to 150% of poverty) were over twice as likely to have worked full-time full-year (66%) than working poor mothers not receiving welfare (30%) and over three-times as likely as mothers who combined work and welfare during the year (20%). Clearly, full-time full-year work lessens the chances, but does not eliminate the chances that a single mother and her children will be poor or receive cash welfare.

Among single mothers who did not work full-time full-year, 63% were poor or received cash welfare in 1999, compared to only 14% who worked full-time full-year (not shown in figures).

Figure 13. Working Single Mothers' Job Attachment, by Welfare and Poverty Status: 1999

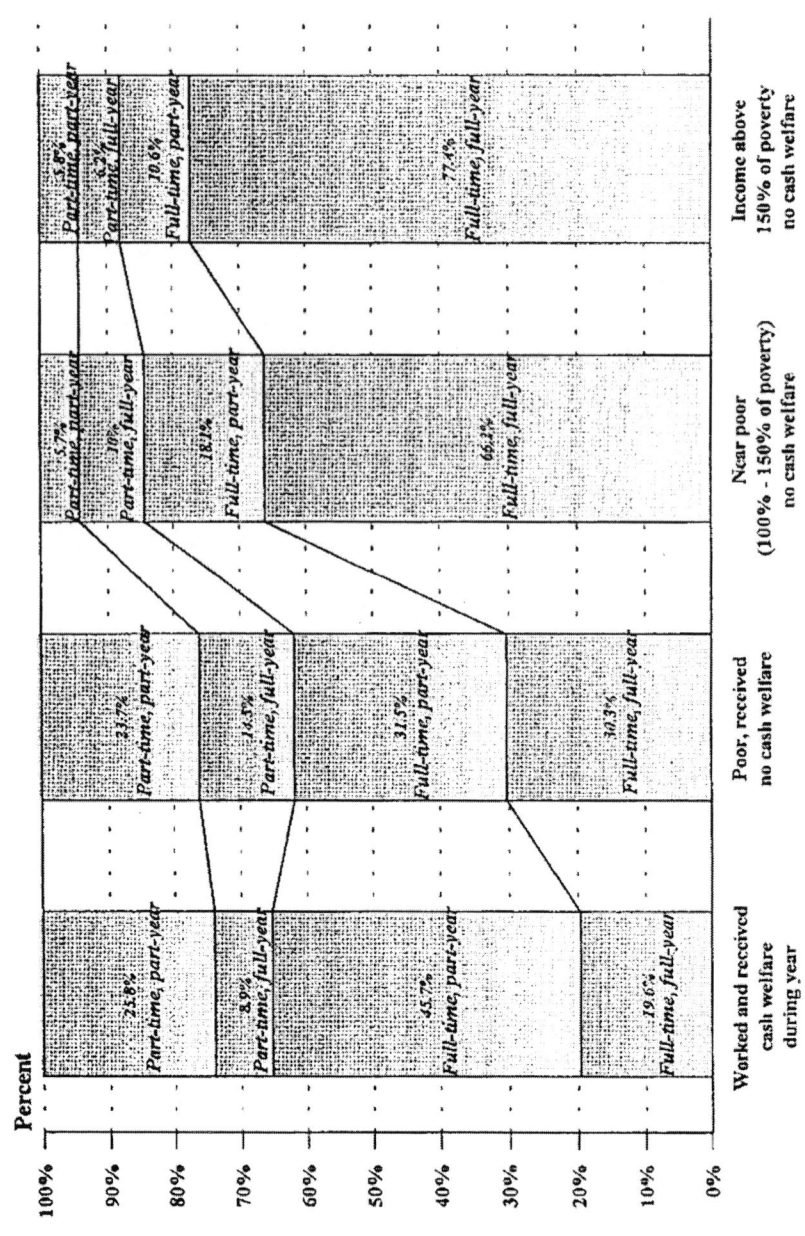

Source: Prepared by the Congressional Research Service (CRS). Based on analysis of U.S. Census Bureau March 1988 to 2000 Current Population Survey (CPS) data.

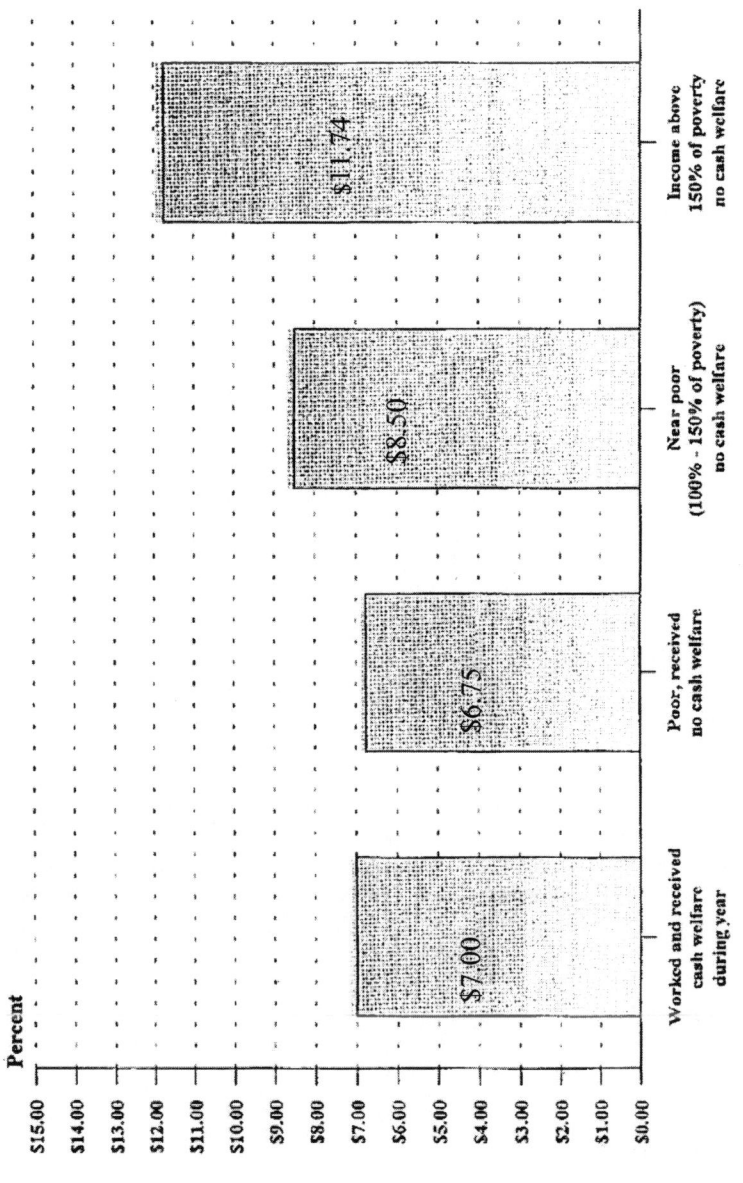

Figure 14. Median Hourly Wage* of Working Single Mothers in March 2000, by Welfare and Poverty Status in 1999

Source: Prepared by the Congressional Research Service (CRS). Based on analysis of U.S. Census Bureau March 1988 to 2000 Current Population Survey (CPS) data.

* Hourly wage for hourly wage workers, and estimated hourly wage equivalent, based on reported gross weekly earnings divided by usual weekly hours worked, for CPS outgoing rotation group (approximately 1/4th of CPS sample).

In March 2000, most working single mothers who are poor or receive cash welfare earned more than the federal statutory minimum wage of $5.15 per hour. Figure 14 shows that in March 2000, there was little difference in the median hourly earnings of single mothers who received welfare during the prior year ($7.00 per hour), and those who were poor but did not receive welfare ($6.75 per hour).[1] Median hourly earnings of working single mothers with incomes just above poverty were $8.50 per hour, $1.50 to $1.75 per hour greater, 22% to 26% higher, than the hourly earnings of mothers who combined work and welfare or who were poor but received no cash welfare during the year.

Absent significant increases in single mothers' job attachment or hourly earnings, income supports in the form of child support, earnings supplements, such as the EITC, food, housing, and medical assistance, as well as cash welfare, are likely to continue to play important roles in addressing the needs of single-mother families. A challenge for these and other approaches will be to reduce basic unmet need and at the same time promote economic self-sufficiency.

---

[1] The CPS asks questions about hourly wage rates of hourly workers for only about one fourth of the CPS sample who are leaving the survey – a group technically referred to as the "outgoing rotation group." (The CPS interviews households for 8 months. After 4 months of interviews, a household leaves the survey for 4 months, and afterwards is interviewed for an additional 4 months, after which the household leaves the survey permanently. In March, selected questions, such as hourly wage rates, are asked only of households who have been in the survey for 4 or 8 months, and will be leaving the survey in the following month (either temporarily or permanently)). The estimates of hourly earnings shown in Figure 14 are based on hourly wages of hourly workers, and for other workers, estimated hourly earnings based on reported gross weekly earnings divided by usual hours worked, among workers in the outgoing rotation group.

Appendix A

CASH WELFARE UNDER-REPORTING ON THE CPS

Figure A-1. AFDC/TANF Cases: CPS versus Administrative Caseload Counts (Annual Monthly Average), 1987 to 1999

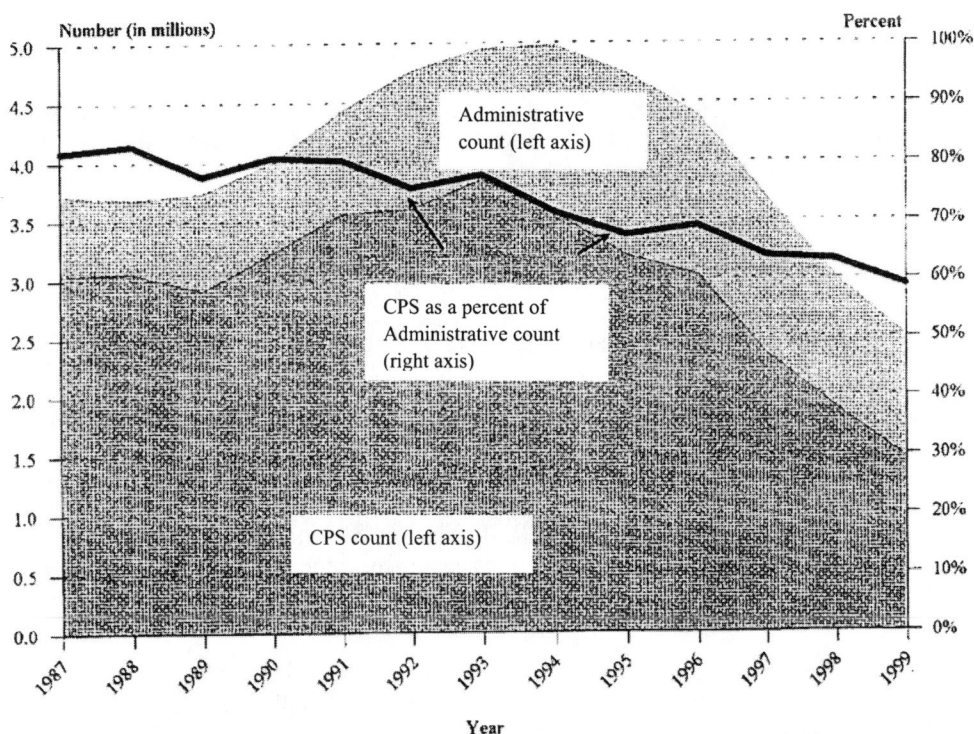

Source: Prepared by the Congressional Research Service (CRS). Based on analysis of U.S. Census Bureau March 1988 to 2000 Current Population Survey (CPS) data and Department of Health and Human Services (DHHS) caseload data.

Figure A-1. Support Table 1. AFDC/TANF Cases: CPS versus Administrative Caseload Counts, Annual Monthly Average, 1987 to 1999 (numbers in millions)

Year	Persons reporting AFDC or TANF receipt on the CPS[a]	AFDC and TANF cases based on administrative data[b]	CPS as a percent of administrative total
1987	3.039	3.719	81.7
1988	3.056	3.691	82.8
1989	2.901	3.738	77.6
1990	3.226	3.995	80.8
1991	3.554	4.434	80.2
1992	3.596	4.765	75.5
1993	3.844	4.949	77.7
1994	3.551	4.974	71.4
1995	3.193	4.741	67.3
1996	3.022	4.387	68.9
1997	2.355	3.690	63.8
1998	1.892	3.000	63.1
1999	1.464	2.496	58.7

Source: Congressional Research Service (CRS) estimates based on U.S. Bureau of the Census March 1988 to 2000 Current Population Survey (CPS) data and U.S. Department of Health and Human Services (DHHS) AFDC and TANF caseload data.

[a] Estimated average monthly number based on number of months CPS respondents indicated they received AFDC or TANF during the year.

[b] Average monthly number of AFDC cases in the 50 states and the District of Columbia.

A comparison of AFDC/TANF administrative statistics and CPS-estimated caseload counts suggests that the CPS undercounts actual cases and that the CPS undercount has worsened in recent years. Figure A-1 shows that from 1987 to 1991, the CPS accounted for roughly 80% of the AFDC administrative caseload count, but by 1999 the CPS was capturing only about 59%.[1] Worsened reporting of cash welfare on the CPS makes it difficult to gauge how much of the drop in welfare receipt among single mothers represents eligible families who do not receive assistance, rather than families who do not report actual welfare aid on the CPS.

---

[1] The CPS estimates are for all adults reporting receipt of AFDC or TANF during the year, converted to an estimate of an annual monthly average, based on the number of months over the year recipients reported receiving assistance. For a detailed discussion of cash welfare under-reporting on the CPS and other surveys see: Bavier, Richard. *Accounting for increases in failure to report AFDC/TANF receipt.* Unpublished manuscript. Washington, D.C. Office of Management and Budget. 2000.

Appendix B

FAMILY INCOME TO POVERTY RATION – CUTOFFS FOR INCOME QUINTILES

Figure B-l shows the income relative to poverty cutoffs for defining the first and second income quintiles depicted in Figures 11 and 12. The dark lines represent the level of family cash income (i.e., the income definition for measuring poverty under the official U.S. Bureau of the Census poverty definition) as a percent of poverty which defines the bottom fifth and bottom two-fifths of single-mother families, ranked by family relative to poverty. The lighter-shaded lines show other income percentiles relative to poverty. The figure shows, for example that the bottom fifth of single-mother families ranked by official cash income relative to poverty had family income below 42% of poverty in 1992; by 1999, the relative income of the bottom fifth of single-mother families increased to having family income below 61% of the poverty line. Similarly, the second-fifth of single-mother families had family income above 42% of poverty but below 85% of poverty in 1992; by 1999, the second-fifth of single mother families had family incomes above 61% of poverty but below 119% of poverty. The figure shows that the bottom 10% of single-mother families has shown little improvement in family income relative to poverty over the 13 year period, ranging from a low of 27% of poverty in 1992, to a high of 32% of poverty in 1999.

Figures B-2 and B-3 are similar to Figure B-l, but depict single-mother families' income rankings based on alternative definitions of income relative to poverty. Figure B-2, for example, ranks families based on family after-tax income (including the EITC) plus food stamps, whereas Figure B-3 ranks families based on household after-tax income plus food stamps, relative to a household poverty income threshold based on household size and composition. In both cases, Figures B-2 and B-3 show comparatively better income position relative to poverty than does Figure B-l, which uses the official poverty income definition. For example, in 1999, the bottom fifth of single-mother families had incomes below 61% of poverty under the official poverty income definition, shown in Figure B-l. When taxes, including the EITC, and food stamps are considered the bottom fifth of single-mother families had incomes below 80% of poverty (shown in Figure B-2), and if household after-tax income and food stamps are counted against a revised household poverty threshold, the bottom 20% of single-mother families have incomes below 90% of poverty (shown in Figure B-3). Although the alternate income definitions also result in improved income standing relative to poverty for the bottom 10% of single-mother families compared to the official poverty income measure, the trend in relative economic well-being for this group is only slightly improved in 1999 compared to its 1992 low under these alternative measures.

Figure B-1. Income to Poverty Percentiles of Mother-Only Families Based on Families Ranked by Family Cash Income Relative to Poverty Income Thresholds, 1987 to 1999

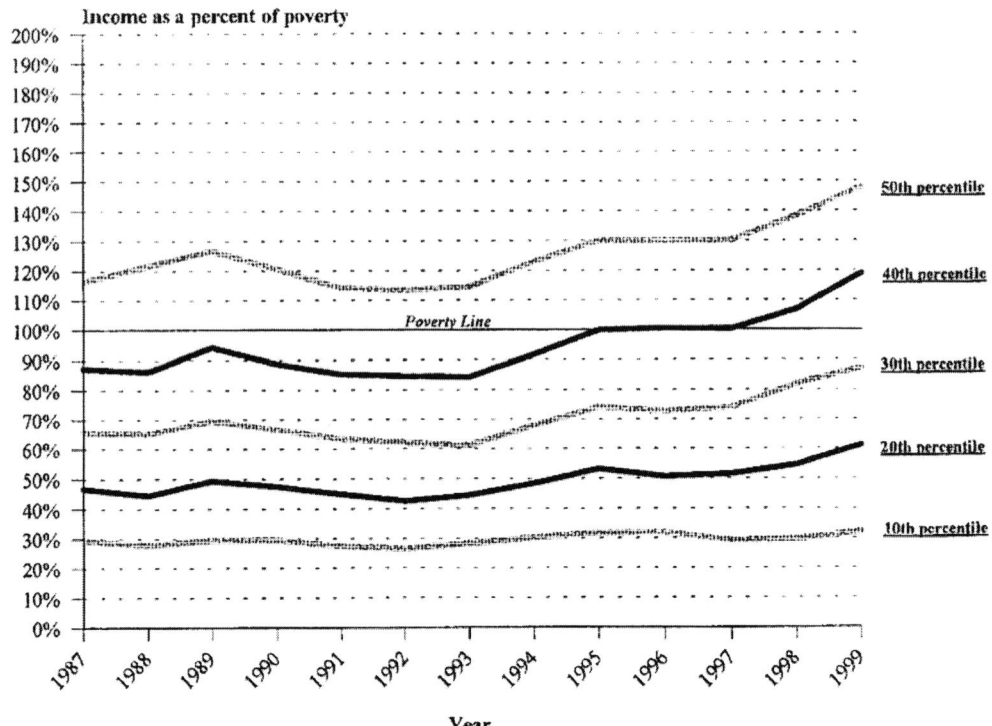

Source: Prepared by the Congressional Research Service (CRS). Based on analysis of U.S. Census Bureau March 1988 to 2000 Current Population Survey (CPS) data.

Figure B-1. Support Table 2. Income to Poverty Percentiles of Mother-Only Families Based Families Ranked by Family Cash Income Relative to Family Poverty Income Thresholds, 1987 to 1999

Year	Income as a percent of poverty defined at each percentile				
	10th %tile	20th %tile	30th %tile	40th %tile	50th %tile
1987	29.3	46.7	65.6	87.2	116.5
1988	27.8	44.5	65.0	86.2	121.7
1989	29.6	49.3	69.5	94.2	126.8
1990	29.6	47.3	66.5	88.8	120.7
1991	27.3	44.9	63.4	85.3	114.2
1992	26.5	42.5	62.0	84.7	113.5
1993	28.2	44.4	61.0	84.2	114.6
1994	30.1	48.2	67.9	91.8	122.9
1995	31.9	53.2	74.3	99.8	130.0
1996	31.9	50.6	72.8	100.5	130.0
1997	29.3	51.4	73.9	100.2	130.3
1998	29.5	54.5	82.0	106.9	138.3
1999	32.1	61.0	87.2	119.0	148.0

Source: Congressional Research Service (CRS) estimates based on analysis of U.S. Bureau of the Census March 1988 to 2000 Current Population Survey (CPS) data.

Figure B-2. Income to Poverty Percentiles of Mother-Only Families Based on Families Ranked by Family After-Tax Income Plus Food Stamps Relative to Family Poverty Income Thresholds, 1987 to 1999

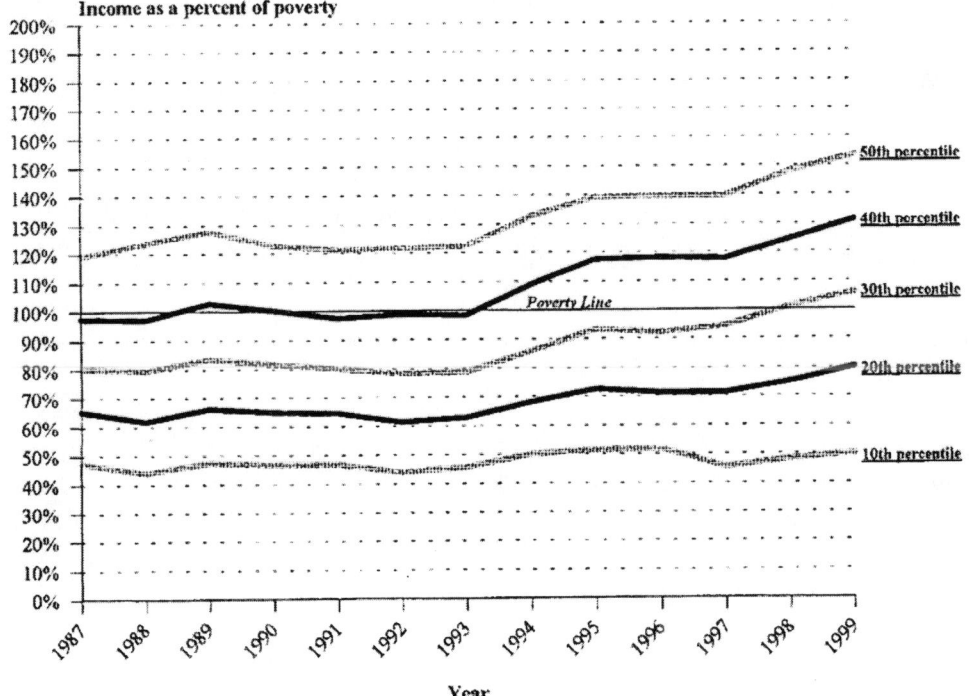

Source: Prepared by the Congressional Research Service (CRS). Based on analysis of U.S. Census Bureau March 1988 to 2000 Current Population Survey (CPS) data.

Figure B-3. Income to Poverty Percentiles of Mother-Only Families Based on Families Ranked by Household After-Tax Income Plus Food Stamps Relative to Household Poverty Income Thresholds, 1987 to 1999

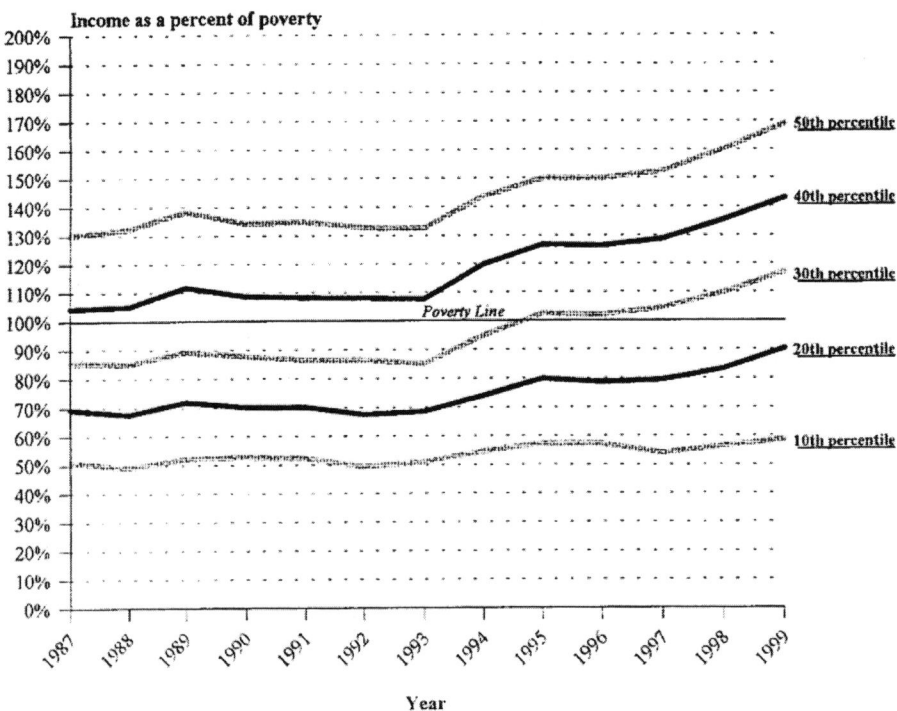

Source: Prepared by the Congressional Research Service (CRS). Based on analysis of U.S. Census Bureau March 1988 to 2000 Current Population Survey (CPS) data.

Figure B-2. Support Table 3. Income to Poverty Percentiles of Mother-Only Families Based on Families Ranked by Family After-Tax Income Plus Food Stamps Relative to Family Poverty Income Thresholds, 1987 to 1999

	Income as a percent of poverty defined at each percentile				
Year	10th %tile	20th %tile	30th %tile	40th %tile	50th %tile
1987	47.2	65.3	80.6	97.5	119.3
1988	43.8	61.8	79.6	97.1	123.7
1989	47.4	66.2	83.5	102.7	127.8
1990	46.7	65.1	81.7	100.2	122.8
1991	46.9	64.5	80.1	97.6	121.3
1992	43.8	61.5	78.4	98.7	121.7
1993	45.7	62.9	78.7	98.2	122.4
1994	50.0	68.2	85.8	108.8	132.6
1995	51.5	72.6	93.3	117.4	139.1
1996	51.8	71.3	92.2	118.1	139.6
1997	45.4	71.4	94.3	117.7	139.7
1998	48.2	75.0	101.1	124.6	148.1
1999	50.1	80.1	105.9	131.2	153.7

Source: Congressional Research Service (CRS) estimates based on analysis of U.S. Bureau of the Census March 1988 to 2000 Current Population Survey (CPS) data.

Figure B-3. Support Table 4. Income to Poverty Percentiles of Mother-Only Families Based on Families Ranked by Household After-Tax Income Plus Food Stamps Relative to Household Poverty Income Thresholds, 1987 to 1999

Year	Income as a percent of poverty defined at each percentile				
	10th %tile	20th %tile	30th %tile	40th %tile	50th %tile
1987	51.1	69.3	85.6	104.5	130.1
1988	49.1	67.5	85.0	105.1	132.2
1989	52.1	71.9	89.1	111.9	138.3
1990	52.8	70.2	87.8	108.7	134.0
1991	52.3	70.1	86.3	108.2	134.7
1992	49.4	67.6	86.3	108.1	132.7
1993	50.9	68.7	84.9	107.6	132.6
1994	54.5	74.0	94.7	119.9	143.6
1995	57.2	79.7	102.4	126.7	149.8
1996	57.2	78.7	102.0	126.3	149.8
1997	54.0	79.4	104.4	128.7	152.3
1998	56.4	83.2	109.8	135.3	160.2
1999	58.6	90.2	117.1	143.0	168.9

Source: Congressional Research Service (CRS) estimates based on analysis of U.S. Bureau of the Census March 1988 to 2000 Current Population Survey (CPS) data.

Appendix C

SUPPORT TABLES

Figure 1. Support Table 5. Single Mothers: Poverty and Cash Welfare Receipt, 1987 to 1999 (in thousands)

Year	Number of mother only families	Number receiving AFDC/TANF	Poor but not receiving AFDC/TANF	Neither poor nor receiving AFDC/TANF
1987	8,193	2,719	1,399	4,076
1988	8,321	2,737	1,380	4,204
1989	8,400	2,537	1,452	4,411
1990	8,745	2,901	1,456	4,387
1991	9,031	3,101	1,554	4,375
1992	9,567	3,300	1,691	4,575
1993	9,860	3,439	1,722	4,700
1994	9,837	3,166	1,754	4,916
1995	9,887	2,862	1,818	5,207
1996	10,052	2,669	1,946	5,437
1997	9,874	2,225	2,211	5,438
1998	9,881	1,872	2,253	5,756
1999	9,741	1,543	2,216	5,981

Source: Congressional Research Service (CRS) estimates based on analysis of U.S. Bureau of the Census March 1988 to 2000 Current Population Survey (CPS) data.

Figure 2. Support Table 6. Welfare, Work and Poverty Status Among Single Mothers, 1987 to 1999

Year	Percent who worked during year	Percent poor ("official definition")	Percent who received AFDC/TANF during the year		
			Total	Did not work during year	Worked during year
1987	67.3	44.7	33.2	21.8	11.4
1988	68.9	43.9	32.9	21.1	11.8
1989	70.1	41.7	30.2	20.1	10.1
1990	69.8	43.7	33.2	20.9	12.3
1991	68.7	45.4	34.3	22.0	12.3
1992	67.2	45.4	34.5	22.2	12.3
1993	68.1	45.2	34.9	21.8	13.1
1994	71.4	42.7	32.2	18.8	13.4
1995	73.0	40.2	28.9	16.5	12.4
1996	75.1	39.8	26.6	14.6	12.0
1997	77.3	40.0	22.5	11.4	11.1
1998	79.6	37.3	18.9	8.2	10.7
1999	82.0	34.0	15.8	6.5	9.3

Source: Congressional Research Service (CRS) estimates based on analysis of U.S. Bureau of the Census March 1988 to 2000 Current Population Survey (CPS) data.

Figure 3. Support Table 7. Employment Rates in March of Single Mothers and Married Mothers by Age of Youngest Child, March 1988 to March 2000 (percent of single mothers employed in March)

Year	Single mothers				Married mothers			
	With a child under age 18	Youngest child under age 3	Youngest child age 3 to 5	Youngest child age 6 to 17	With a child under age 18	Youngest child under age 3	Youngest child age 3 to 5	Youngest child age 6 to 17
1988	57.4	35.1	52.9	69.1	61.8	50.7	58.1	69.6
1989	58.2	37.9	53.1	70.0	63.0	51.4	60.8	70.6
1990	60.3	38.0	61.0	70.9	63.4	52.7	60.9	70.8
1991	58.1	36.6	55.7	70.2	63.1	52.7	60.5	70.5
1992	57.3	35.2	54.1	69.8	63.9	53.1	59.4	71.9
1993	57.3	35.1	54.8	70.1	63.9	53.2	59.4	71.9
1994	58.0	37.7	55.2	69.3	65.5	56.0	61.2	72.6
1995	61.1	43.1	58.6	70.5	67.1	57.4	63.9	73.4
1996	63.5	44.7	60.4	72.9	67.6	58.2	63.3	74.2
1997	65.6	51.5	64.3	72.0	68.5	58.3	64.4	75.2
1998	68.8	54.8	63.7	76.4	67.9	58.3	64.1	74.2
1999	70.7	55.8	69.8	77.1	67.9	57.0	63.1	75.1
2000	72.8	59.1	72.7	78.5	68.4	56.8	66.0	75.0

Source: Congressional Research Service (CRS) estimates based on analysis of U.S. Census Bureau March 1988 to March 2000 Current Population Survey (CPS) data.

Figures 4 and 5. Support Table 8. Single-Mother Family Cash Welfare Recipiency Rates, by Pre-Transfer Income Poverty Status*, 1987 to 1999

	All single-mother families		Single-mother families with pre-transfer income below poverty										
			Total		0$ in pre-transfer income		Pre-transfer income below 25% of poverty		Pre-transfer income from 25% to below 50% of poverty		Pre-transfer income from 50% to below 100% of poverty		
Year	Number (in 1,000s)	AFDC/TANF recipiency rate (%)	Number (in 1,000s)	AFDC/TANF recipiency rate (%)	Number (in 1,000s)	AFDC/TANF recipiency rate (%)	Number (in 1,000s)	AFDC/TANF recipiency rate (%)	Number (in 1,000s)	AFDC/TANF recipiency rate (%)	Number (in 1,000s)	AFDC/TANF recipiency rate (%)
1987	8,193	33.2	3,820	63.4	1,020	88.7	1,003	77.0	609	59.9	1,179	31.8
1988	8,321	32.9	3,816	63.8	1,055	89.5	970	73.8	723	53.3	1,064	36.8
1989	8,400	30.2	3,672	60.5	1,022	85.7	871	72.8	593	55.6	1,183	32.2
1990	8,745	33.2	4,029	63.8	1,142	88.4	909	75.1	677	60.4	1,294	35.9
1991	9,031	34.3	4,276	63.6	1,215	87.3	973	79.2	689	63.6	1,391	32.4
1992	9,567	34.5	4,536	62.7	1,159	85.2	1,102	73.5	819	56.4	1,450	40.1
1993	9,860	34.9	4,679	63.2	1,104	84.7	1,180	78.3	909	60.0	1,477	37.3
1994	9,837	32.2	4,474	60.8	961	82.0	1,058	75.2	835	61.0	1,618	38.7
1995	9,887	28.9	4,181	56.5	753	80.3	941	73.2	862	59.7	1,625	34.2
1996	10,052	26.6	4,168	53.3	776	76.6	838	71.9	994	52.2	1,560	32.4
1997	9,874	22.5	4,119	46.3	685	68.4	846	62.6	843	46.2	1,736	30.0
1998	9,881	18.9	3,834	41.2	554	61.3	778	55.7	806	45.1	1,682	26.2
1999	9,741	15.8	3,442	35.6	378	56.5	711	46.0	736	37.9	1,617	25.2

Source: Congressional Research Service (CRS) estimates based on analysis of U.S. Bureau of the Census March 1988 to March 2000 Current Population Survey (CPS) data.

* Family poverty status based on cash income other than cash welfare.

Figure 6. Support Table 9. Food Stamp Recipiency Rates among Single-Mother Families, by Household Income Relative to Poverty, 1987 to 1999

Year	All single-mother families		Household income below 130% of poverty					
			Total		Household income less than 50% of poverty		Household income from 50% to below 130% of poverty	
	Number (in 1,000s)	Food stamp recipiency rate	Number (in 1,000s)	Food stamp recipiency rate	Number (in 1,000s)	Food stamp recipiency rate	Number (in 1,000s)	Food stamp recipiency rate
1987	8,193	35.8	4,063	65.7	1,595	76.1	2,469	59.0
1988	8,321	36.3	4,121	65.7	1,706	75.1	2,414	59.0
1989	8,400	33.9	3,917	63.7	1,466	76.9	2,451	55.8
1990	8,745	37.1	4,265	68.4	1,651	79.4	2,614	61.4
1991	9,031	39.1	4,472	68.8	1,736	79.9	2,736	61.7
1992	9,567	41.1	4,756	70.9	1,970	79.8	2,787	64.5
1993	9,860	42.5	4,990	70.8	1,955	80.7	3,034	64.4
1994	9,837	40.2	4,673	70.9	1,786	80.3	2,887	65.1
1995	9,887	37.2	4,494	66.5	1,539	77.3	2,955	60.9
1996	10,052	35.8	4,545	65.0	1,633	76.8	2,912	58.4
1997	9,874	32.4	4,392	61.5	1,642	73.1	2,750	54.6
1998	9,881	29.8	4,193	56.7	1,491	69.5	2,703	49.6
1999	9,741	24.9	3,746	51.5	1,274	63.3	2,472	45.4

Source: Congressional Research Service (CRS) estimates based on analysis of U.S. Bureau of the Census March 1988 to 2000 Current Population Survey (CPS) data.

Figure 7. Support Table 10. Poor Single Mothers: Work and Welfare Status During the Year, 1987 to 1999

Year	Number of poor single mothers (in 1,000s)	Percent					
		Received cash welfare during year	Received cash welfare but did not work during year	Combined work and welfare over the year	Worked at any time during the year	Worked but did not receive cash welfare at any time during the year	Neither worked, nor received welfare during the year
1987	3,661	61.8	43.3	18.5	42.2	23.7	14.5
1988	3,650	62.2	43.0	19.2	43.5	24.3	13.5
1989	3,506	58.6	42.7	15.9	43.1	27.2	14.2
1990	3,821	61.9	41.4	20.5	46.0	25.5	12.6
1991	4,101	62.1	43.3	18.8	44.3	25.5	12.5
1992	4,339	61.0	42.1	18.9	43.6	24.7	14.3
1993	4,456	61.4	41.5	19.8	44.3	24.5	14.1
1994	4,203	58.3	37.8	20.5	47.3	26.8	14.9
1995	3,971	54.2	34.2	20.0	49.7	29.7	16.1
1996	4,005	51.4	31.1	20.3	52.6	32.2	16.4
1997	3,946	44.0	24.5	19.5	57.8	38.3	17.7
1998	3,685	38.9	19.2	19.7	60.4	40.7	20.4
1999	3,314	33.1	15.4	17.8	64.3	46.5	20.3

Source: Congressional Research Service (CRS) estimates based on analysis of U.S. Bureau of the Census March 1988 to 2000 Current Population Survey (CPS) data.

Figure 8. Support Table 11. Effects of Earnings, Transfers, and Taxes on Family Poverty and Household Low-Income Status on Single Mothers, 1987 to 1999

Year	Family earned income only	Preceding column +: Family cash income other than welfare	Preceding column +: Family cash welfare ("official poverty income")	Preceding column +: Family food stamps	Preceding column +: Family EITC less FICA and income taxes	Preceding column +: Household cash income + food stamps + EITC less FICA and income taxes
1987	53.9	46.6	44.7	42.3	41.1	38.2
1988	53.8	45.9	43.9	42.2	41.3	37.9
1989	52.2	43.7	41.7	39.7	39.2	35.5
1990	53.8	46.1	43.7	41.5	39.9	36.1
1991	55.2	47.4	45.4	42.8	41.3	37.0
1992	55.3	47.4	45.4	42.5	40.6	36.5
1993	56.2	47.4	45.2	42.7	40.7	36.8
1994	53.9	45.5	42.7	39.8	36.5	32.1
1995	51.0	42.3	40.2	36.9	32.5	29.2
1996	49.8	41.5	39.8	37.1	32.9	29.3
1997	50.6	41.7	40.0	37.7	32.6	28.3
1998	47.9	38.8	37.3	35.2	29.7	26.2
1999	43.6	35.3	34.0	32.2	27.5	23.6

Source: Congressional Research Service (CRS) estimates based on analysis of U.S. Bureau of the Census March 1988 to 2000 Current Population Survey (CPS) data.

Figure 9. Support Table 12. Poverty Gap Percentiles* Based on Cash Income for Poor Single-Mother Families, 1987 to 1999

Year	Bottom 20%	Bottom 40%	Median (50th percentile)	Top 40%	Top 20%
1987	27.2	43.4	51.1	60.0	78.2
1988	26.1	40.7	48.1	57.1	74.9
1989	25.6	42.1	50.9	58.9	77.1
1990	27.4	43.0	50.0	58.9	76.1
1991	25.6	42.5	50.5	58.6	75.2
1992	24.2	39.3	48.0	56.6	75.1
1993	26.2	41.0	49.0	56.7	73.6
1994	27.6	43.8	50.7	58.7	76.3
1995	27.7	45.8	53.3	60.3	79.7
1996	27.7	43.5	50.5	58.9	77.7
1997	22.3	42.9	51.3	60.7	78.6
1998	22.6	42.5	51.5	60.3	81.2
1999	23.4	43.1	52.8	62.0	80.1

Source: Congressional Research Service (CRS) estimates based on analysis of U.S. Bureau of the Census March 1988 to 2000 Current Population Survey (CPS).

*Poor families' cash income as a percent of families' poverty thresholds.

Figure 10. Support Table 13. Poverty Gap Percentiles* Based on Cash Income, Food Stamps, and Net Taxes Including the EITC for Poor Single-Mother Families, 1987 to 1999

Year	Bottom 20%	Bottom 40%	Median (50th percentile)	Top 40%	Top 20%
1987	43.1	59.1	66.1	72.7	85.4
1988	37.7	55.9	63.8	71.1	85.0
1989	40.1	58.6	65.4	72.3	85.4
1990	41.1	58.9	65.1	71.3	84.8
1991	42.6	59.3	65.6	72.1	84.8
1992	38.6	56.0	61.9	68.6	83.0
1993	40.5	56.7	63.4	69.6	82.6
1994	42.7	59.0	65.1	71.1	84.3
1995	40.3	58.5	65.2	71.4	85.0
1996	41.2	58.0	64.0	70.8	84.3
1997	34.7	54.3	62.8	70.3	85.0
1998	30.7	53.9	61.5	68.4	84.6
1999	31.3	53.1	61.6	70.0	84.8

Source: Congressional Research Service (CRS) estimates based on analysis of U.S. Bureau of the Census March 1988 to 2000 Current Population Survey (CPS).

*Poor families' cash income as a percent of families' poverty thresholds.

Figure 11. Support Table 14. Bottom Quintile* of Single Mother Families: Average Annual Income by Source, 1987 to 1999 (in 1999 dollars)

Year	Federal and state income taxes and FICA taxes	AFDC, TANF, General Assistance	Supplemental Security Income (SSI)	Food stamps (market value)	Child support and alimony	Other income	Family earnings (net of taxes)	EITC	Total income net of taxes
1987	-$79	$2,739	$106	$2,249	$226	$405	$806	$101	$6,633
1988	-$85	$2,431	$82	$1,953	$209	$357	$960	$115	$6,107
1989	-$71	$2,558	$99	$1,121	$217	$455	$806	$107	$6,362
1990	-$76	$2,713	$90	$2,170	$185	$318	$860	$113	$6,449
1991	-$62	$2,669	$91	$2,374	$158	$285	$704	$112	$6,393
1992	-$59	$2,322	$148	$2,264	$199	$370	$691	$115	$6,108
1993	-$60	$2,441	$153	$2,213	$218	$446	$665	$118	$6,254
1994	-$84	$2,541	$239	$2,476	$251	$384	$988	$274	$7,151
1995	-$103	$2,297	$279	$2,139	$288	$449	$1,242	$412	$7,107
1996	-$123	$2,039	$235	$2,098	$322	$416	$1,427	$529	$7,067
1997	-$105	$1,818	$204	$1,978	$260	$607	$1,234	$468	$6,570
1998	-$146	$1,441	$276	$1,747	$220	$586	$1,648	$641	$6,560
1999	-$184	$1,184	$301	$1,509	$342	$609	$2,107	$784	$6,837

Source: Congressional Research Service (CRS) estimates based on analysis of U.S. Bureau of the Census March 1988 to 2000 Current Population Survey (CPS).

* Quintiles based on ranking of ratios of family cash pre-tax income relative to poverty. Taxes include federal and state income taxes and FICA taxes.

Figure 12. Support Table 15. Second Quintile* of Single Mother Families: Average Annual Income by Source, 1987 to 1999 (in 1999 dollars)

Year	Federal and state income taxes and FICA taxes	AFDC, TANF, General Assistance	Supplemental Security Income (SSI)	Food stamps (market value)	Child support and alimony	Other income	Family earnings (net of taxes)	EITC	Total income net of taxes
1987	-$286	$4,249	$486	$1,670	$406	$1,650	$3,437	$379	$12,278
1988	-$293	$4,064	$441	$1,669	$358	$1,510	$3,400	$392	$11,834
1989	-$379	$3,777	$560	$1,445	$463	$1,443	$4,379	$482	$12,548
1990	-$385	$3,719	$458	$1,754	$463	$1,462	$4,112	$471	$12,439
1991	-$319	$3,662	$470	$1,837	$389	$1,404	$3,629	$561	$11,951
1992	-$312	$3,330	$452	$1,765	$516	$1,408	$3,520	$556	$11,547
1993	-$289	$3,434	$688	$1,763	$454	$1,275	$3,286	$548	$11,648
1994	-$383	$2,847	$804	$1,656	$580	$1,458	$4,317	$1,092	$12,755
1995	-$540	$2,494	$929	$1,694	$607	$1,808	$5,723	$1,497	$14,752
1996	-$503	$2,127	$794	$1,427	$620	$1,668	$5,400	$1,587	$13,623
1997	-$543	$1,616	$759	$1,254	$747	$1,646	$6,130	$1,900	$14,053
1998	-$685	$1,203	$847	$1,050	$544	$1,689	$7,491	$2,125	$14,948
1999	-$824	$906	$755	$761	$701	$1,519	$8,770	$2,267	$15,679

Source: Congressional Research Service (CRS) estimates based on analysis of U.S. Bureau of the Census March 1988 to 2000 Current Population Survey (CPS).

* Quintiles based on ranking of ratios of family cash pre-tax income relative to poverty. Taxes include federal and state income taxes and FICA taxes.

INDEX

#

1996 welfare law, 2, 32

A

AFDC benefits, 3
after-tax income, 27, 39
Aid to Families with Dependent Children (AFDC), vi, 1, 2, 3, 5, 9, 28, 29, 32, 37, 38, 45, 46, 48, 53, 54
alimony, 28, 53, 54
anti-poverty effectiveness, 22, 23
average annual income, 28
average net earnings, 29

B

benefit standards, 1
block grant program, vi, 1

C

cash assistance, 3, 9, 11, 22, 29
cash income poverty measure, 25
cash welfare, vi, 1, 2, 3, 5, 6, 11, 12, 13, 15, 17, 19, 20, 22, 23, 28, 29, 32, 33, 36, 38, 48, 50, 51
cash welfare caseloads, 1, 2, 32
cash welfare receipt, 5, 6, 32
cash welfare recipiency rates, 11, 12
Child Care and Development Block Grant (CCDBG), 2
child care assistance, 2
child support, 28, 36
children, vi, 1, 2, 5, 9, 12, 22, 32, 33

Congressional Research Service (CRS), 1, 2, 3, 6, 7, 10, 12, 13, 14, 16, 21, 26, 27, 30, 31, 32, 34, 35, 37, 38, 40, 41, 42, 43, 45, 46, 47, 48, 49, 50, 51, 52, 53, 54
CPS undercount, 38
Current Population Survey (CPS), v, vi, 1, 3, 4, 5, 6, 7, 10, 12, 13, 14, 16, 17, 21, 23, 26, 27, 30, 31, 32, 33, 34, 35, 36, 37, 38, 40, 41, 42, 43, 45, 46, 47, 48, 49, 50, 51, 52, 53, 54

D

Department of Health and Human Services (DHHS), 2, 37, 38

E

Earned Income Tax Credit (EITC), vii, 2, 3, 9, 10, 19, 20, 22, 23, 25, 27, 28, 29, 32, 36, 39, 51, 52, 53, 54
earnings supplements, 36
economic well-being, vi, 1, 19, 28, 40
economies of scale, 20
employment rates, 9

F

family after-tax income, 39
family cash income, 19, 23, 39
family composition, 3
family earnings, 19, 20
family income, vi, vii, 1, 4, 19, 25, 28, 29, 32, 39
family poverty income thresholds, 20
family size, 5, 19, 20, 25
Family Support Act of 1988, vi, 1
federal entitlement program, vi, 1

federally-funded assistance, 1
female-headed families, vi, 1, 12
financial need, 11
food stamp benefits, vii, 12, 29
Food Stamp Program, 12
food stamp recipiency rates, 12
food stamps, 19, 20, 22, 23, 25, 27, 28, 29, 32, 39, 51
full-time schedules, 33

G

General Assistance (GA), 28, 29, 53, 54
government assistance, vi, 1

H

hourly earnings, 36
household low-income line, 23
household low-income threshold, 20
household members, 17, 19, 20, 22, 23

I

income, vii, 3, 5, 11, 12, 13, 17, 19, 20, 22, 23, 25, 26, 28, 29, 30, 31, 32, 36, 39, 48, 49, 51, 52, 53, 54
income distribution, 28
income sharing, 20
income taxes, 20, 23, 28, 30, 31, 51, 53, 54
inflation, 3, 32
in-kind benefits, 19

L

low-income families, vi, 1, 2, 23
low-income households, 12

M

marriage, vi, 1, 20
median family income, 25
minimum wage, 3, 9, 32, 36

N

needy families, vi, 1
net earnings, 28, 29
non-family members' income, 23

O

official poverty measure, 17, 19, 20

P

payroll taxes, 20, 28
Personal Responsibility and Work Opportunity Reconciliation Act (PRWORA), vi, 1
policy interventions, 2, 3, 32
post-tax, 23
poverty, vi, 1, 2, 3, 5, 6, 11, 12, 13, 15, 19, 20, 22, 23, 25, 26, 27, 28, 29, 30, 31, 32, 33, 36, 39, 41, 42, 43, 48, 49, 51, 52, 53, 54
poverty cutoffs, 39
poverty gap, 25
poverty line, 19, 22, 23, 39
poverty rate, 6, 15, 22, 23, 25
poverty ratios, 28
poverty status, vi, 3, 5, 19, 24, 32, 48
poverty threshold, 5, 19, 20, 22, 25, 26, 27, 40, 52
public assistance, 28
public housing, 19

R

rate of decline, 15
recipiency rates, 11

S

sanction policies, 17
school lunches, 19
self-sufficiency, 36
single mothers, vi, 3, 5, 6, 9, 10, 11, 15, 17, 19, 20, 22, 23, 25, 28, 29, 32, 33, 36, 38, 47, 50
single-mother families, vi, 2, 12, 25, 28, 29, 32, 36, 39, 48, 49
social security, 19
state programs, 1, 2
Supplemental Security Income (SSI), 28, 53, 54

T

TANF benefits, 3
Temporary Assistance for Needy Families (TANF), vi, 1, 3, 5, 9, 22, 28, 32, 37, 38, 45, 46, 48, 53, 54

U

U.S. Bureau of the Census, 1, 3, 20, 22, 38, 39, 41, 42, 43, 45, 46, 48, 49, 50, 51, 52, 53, 54
unemployment compensation, 19
United States, iv

W

welfare caseloads, vi, 2, 32
welfare dependency, vii, 33
welfare diversion, 17
welfare policy, 1, 2, 3, 19
welfare reform, vi, 1, 2, 15
welfare system, 9, 32
work and welfare status, 15
work bonus, 2, 23, 29
work rates, 23
work requirements, 2, 9, 23, 32
workers compensation, 19